D0344096

MARY FORD
BISCUIT RECIPES

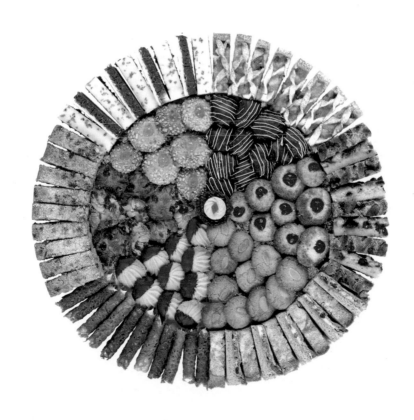

AUTHOR

Mary Ford is an extremely well known name in cake artistry. She is a master cake decorator and teacher. Her step-by-step cake artistry books have sold over 600,000 copies worldwide. However, at heart Mary is concerned with a much wider field. Having run her own bakery business for many years, she remains an enthusiastic home-baker. This passionate interest resulted in her hugely successful book 'Cake Recipes'. This new book on baking reflects Mary's belief that anyone can bake, and that nothing beats the flavour of freshly made biscuits and traybakes. Her unique step-by-step teaching method, and practical hints, means that anyone can benefit from her many years of experience.

ACKNOWLEDGEMENTS

Many thanks to:

CARMEL KEENS who is the Senior Home Economist for Tate & Lyle Sugars. Carmel is a highly respected, and knowledgeable, figure in cookery circles. Her expertise is wide ranging, covering everything from cake decoration, recipe testing, new product development, to budget meals and health education in schools. She is sugar adviser to cookery editors, having produced many of the Tate & Lyle Sugars recipe leaflets and booklets. She is involved in travelling the country to attend trade shows and many major food exhibitions.

R & W SCOTT LTD., Carluke, Scotland for providing all the chocolate used in this book.

PRESTIGE Group UK PLC, 23-26 High Street, Egham, Surrey for their continued co-operation and for supplying cake tins, cookware and decorating items used in this book.

Published 1995 by Mary Ford Publications Ltd. 99 Spring Road, Tyseley, Birmingham, B11 3DJ, U.K.

Typesetting: RussDesign & Production, Salisbury. Colour Separation: Next Graphic Limited, Hong Kong. ISBN 0 9462429 50 2

CONTENTS

3

SUGAR

Sugar, an essential ingredient in the kitchen, originates in the giant grass-like sugar cane which grows in tropical climates such as the Caribbean, Mauritius and Fiji. It is a flavour enhancer, preservative and natural sweetener as well as contributing to the texture of food.

Sugar can aptly be described as 'a taste of sunshine' because it is manufactured in plants as a direct result of the sun's energy, through a process known as photosynthesis. However, whilst all plants make sugars, commercially produced sugars are extracted only from sugar cane and sugar beet.
The extraction process used by Tate & Lyle removes undesirable impurities and produces the characteristic crystalline structure without the addition of any artificial colourings, flavourings or preservatives.

Nutritionally brown and white sugars are virtually identical, but the distinctive colour and flavour of brown sugar arises from molasses, which is the syrup remaining after all the sugar has been removed from the cane juice. When manufacturing white sugar, the molasses is completely removed whilst the different brown sugars contain more, or less, of the syrup depending on the flavour and colour required.
Therefore, careful selection of the type of sugar used can greatly enhance the finished taste and texture.

Icing Sugar: The finest of all sugars. It dissolves rapidly and is especially used in making icings, smooth toppings, confectionery, meringues and cake frostings. Apart from decorating cakes, icing sugar is perfect for sweetening cold drinks and uncooked desserts, as its fine texture makes it easy to dissolve.

Granulated Sugar: Granulated sugar has a very pure crystal and is an ideal boiling sugar. It can be used for sweetening tea, coffee, sprinkling over cereals or frosting cakes and glasses for decoration.

Caster Sugar: Caster sugar is a free flowing sugar with very fine crystals. Excellent for use in baking cakes and other baked goods as the fine white grains ensure smooth blending and an even texture.

Lyle's Golden Syrup: Golden syrup is a partially inverted syrup produced from intermediate refinery sugar liquors when they are heated in the presence of an acid. It is an ideal sweetener and can be used in cooking and baking to add bulk, texture and taste.

Lyle's Black Treacle: Black treacle is a dark, viscous liquid with a characteristic flavour. It is obtained from cane molasses, a by product of sugar refining.

Demerara Sugar: This sugar has a golden colour with a unique flavour that makes it particularly popular in coffee. The grain is larger than granulated and is ideal for decorating biscuits and cakes, sprinkling over desserts and making crunchy toppings.

Light Brown Soft Sugar: This sugar is fine grained, creamy golden in colour and has a mild syrup flavour. It is best used when creamed with butter or margarine in any recipe that requires a deeper, richer colour and fuller flavour.

Dark Brown Soft Sugar: This sugar is darker with a strong flavour and is ideal for rich fruit cakes, gingerbread, spiced teabreads and puddings.

INTRODUCTION

I was delighted by the response to the publication of "Cake Recipes" and received numerous letters asking for a follow-up title. I have deliberately continued the successful step-by-step layout adopted in the previous book in this "Biscuit & Traybake Recipes" title and have incorporated the "Mary's Tips" section which has been a popular feature.

As with "Cake Recipes", I have collected my favourite biscuit and traybake recipes gathered over the years into one book. The recipes selected cater for all tastes and levels of experience in home baking. I have included many ideas which are suitable for children to make, watched over by an adult.

The recipes can be used to produce biscuits and traybakes for the traditional mid morning break or in the afternoon. However, a number of the recipes are suitable for different occasions such as lunchboxes, picnics or as a dessert. The crisp digestive biscuits could easily accompany cheese for an instant snack.

Additions such as cheese, crisps and bacon produce an interesting variety of tastes and textures from smooth to crunchy. A number of the recipes incorporate the simple to use Scotbloc topping which is generally available in supermarkets and smaller shops. The range of toppings and decorations currently available provides ample opportunity for you to add your own originality to the recipe.

In producing this book, I have worked closely with Carmel Keens (Tate & Lyle's home Economist) and I pay tribute to her help in testing and helping with the recipes in this book.

All the recipes can be made with the most basic kitchen equipment. If you do not have exactly the right size of tin, you can vary the shape, so long as the overall area remains the same. In the same way the variety of cutter shapes can be used to add your own improvisation to the finished product.

I am sure you agree that no commercially produced biscuit can have quite the same taste and texture as a recipe made in your own kitchen or just out of the oven. I hope you will get as much enjoyment out of these recipes as I have and they provide many happy hours of baking and eating.

PASSION FRUIT SQUARES

INGREDIENTS
Makes 24

Metric		Imperial
	2 eggs, size 3	
85g	Light brown soft sugar	3oz
85g	Butter melted	3oz
85g	Carrots, peeled and grated	3oz
85g	Banana, mashed	3oz
5ml	Cinnamon	1tsp
5ml	Nutmeg	1tsp
5ml	All spice	1tsp
60g	Walnuts, chopped	2oz
115g	Wholemeal flour	4oz
5ml	Baking powder	1tsp

TOPPING

115g	Quark	4oz
125ml	Whipping cream	¼pt
	1 passion fruit (optional)	

DECORATION

Small carrots made from sugarpaste or almond paste

BAKING TIN

Greased and lined with greaseproof paper 18 x 28cm (7 x 11in) shallow baking tin.

BAKING

Preheated oven, 190°C, 375°F
or gas mark 5
Middle shelf
20 minutes or until firm to touch

1. Whisk together the egg and sugar until thick and creamy, then whisk in the melted butter. Add the carrots, banana, spices and chopped walnuts and mix together thoroughly.

2. Sift together the flour and baking powder then gently fold into the mixture until well blended. Pour the mixture into the tin, spread evenly.

3. When baked, leave in tin for 10 minutes then turn out to cool. Whisk quark and cream together, then add scooped out passion fruit. Spread over top and cut into squares.

PEANUT CRISPS

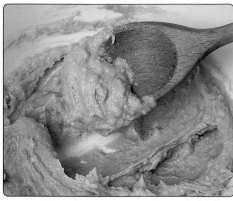

1. *Thoroughly beat together the margarine, sugar, syrup and peanut butter.*

2. *Work in the sifted flour and oatmeal. Dissolve the bicarbonate of soda in the hot water and stir into the mixture to form a soft dough.*

INGREDIENTS
Makes 20

Metric		Imperial
60g	Margarine	2oz
60g	Light brown soft sugar	2oz
60g	Lyle's golden syrup	2oz
115g	Crunchy peanut butter	4oz
85g	Plain flour, sifted	3oz
30g	Medium oatmeal	1oz
1.25ml	Bicarbonate of soda	¼tsp
15ml	Hot water	1tbsp

DECORATION

A little medium oatmeal

BAKING TRAYS

Well greased baking trays.

BAKING

Preheated oven, 180°C or 360°F
or gas mark 4
Middle Shelf
15 minutes or until golden brown

Mary's Tips

It is essential to measure the bicarbonate of soda accurately
to ensure perfect results.

3. *Mould the mixture into a long roll, cut into 20 pieces then mould into rounds. Space apart on trays, flatten and sprinkle with a little oatmeal then bake.*

FRUIT and NUT BARS

INGREDIENTS
Makes 24

Metric		Imperial
225g	Hazelnuts	8oz
225g	Dates	8oz
115g	Glacé cherries	4oz
5ml	Vanilla essence	1tsp
	2 eggs, size 2	
200g	Soft light brown sugar	7oz
60g	Plain flour	2oz
5ml	Baking powder	1tsp

DECORATION

Icing sugar for dusting

BAKING TIN

Well greased 18 x 28cm (7 x 11in) shallow baking tin.

BAKING

Preheated oven, 180°C or 360°F or gas mark 4
Middle Shelf
Approximately 40-45 minutes

Mary's Tips

These bars improve with keeping.
Store them in an airtight tin.

1. Chop the hazelnuts, dates and cherries then mix together in a bowl with the essence.

2. Whisk the eggs and sugar together until light and fluffy. Stir in the mixed fruit.

3. Sift the flour and baking powder together and fold into the mixture until well blended. Spread into the tin and bake. After baking, cut into bars whilst still warm.

OATY JACKS

1. Melt the margarine in a saucepan over low heat then transfer to a bowl. Stir in the sugar and oats.

2. Spoon the mixture into the greased tin then level and bake.

3. After baking, leave to cool for 5 minutes then cut into squares. When cold, dip each piece into melted chocolate and leave to set on non-stick paper.

INGREDIENTS
Makes 16

Metric		Imperial
85g	Margarine	3oz
85g	Light brown soft sugar	3oz
115g	Rolled oats	4oz

DECORATION

115g	Milk or plain Scotbloc or Chocolat	4oz

BAKING TIN

Well greased 20.5cm (8in) square, shallow baking tin.

BAKING

Preheated oven, 170°C or 340°F or gas mark 3
Middle Shelf
30-35 minutes

Mary's Tips

These delicious bars are a lunch box favourite.
For a less rich treat, do not dip into the chocolate.

CURRY TWISTS

INGREDIENTS
Makes 48

Metric		Imperial
85g	Wholemeal self-raising flour	3oz
85g	Self-raising flour, sifted	3oz
	Pinch of salt	
5ml	Curry powder	1tsp
115g	Margarine	4oz
5ml	Dark brown soft sugar	1tsp
15ml	Sesame seeds	1tbsp
	1 egg yolk	
15-30ml	Milk	1-2tbsp

TOPPING

	Milk to glaze	
15-30ml	Sesame seeds	1-2tbsp

BAKING TRAYS

Well greased baking trays.

BAKING

Preheated oven, 190°C, 375°F
or gas mark 5
Middle shelf
15 minutes or until golden brown

1. Place wholemeal flour, white flour, salt and curry powder in a bowl. Rub in the margarine until mixture resembles breadcrumbs. Stir in the brown sugar and sesame seeds.

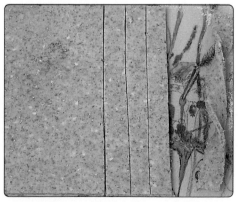

2. Mix in the egg yolk and sufficient milk to make a fairly soft, pliable dough. Roll out on lightly floured surface and cut narrow strips and carefully twist one at a time.

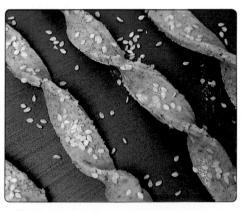

3. Place onto the tray and brush with milk then sprinkle with sesame seeds and bake. Leave on the trays to cool slightly before placing onto wire trays.

JAM BANDITS

INGREDIENTS
Makes 12

Metric		Imperial
225g	Plain flour	8oz
5ml	Baking powder	1tsp
10ml	Ground cinnamon	2tsp
115g	Butter	4oz
85g	Lyle's golden syrup	3oz
	1 egg yolk	

FILLING

Jam or preserve of choice

DECORATION

Icing sugar for dusting

BAKING TIN

Well greased 20.5cm (8in) square, shallow baking tin.

BAKING

Preheated oven, 190°C, 375°F
or gas mark 5
Middle shelf
30 minutes

Mary's Tips

Rinse measures and spoons
in hot water before use,
then syrup can be scraped
off cleanly without waste.

1. Sift together the flour, baking powder and cinnamon. Rub in the butter until breadcrumb texture is formed.

2. Mix in the syrup and yolk to form a smooth dough. Divide the dough in half and then roll out and fit one portion evenly into the tin.

3. Spread a generous amount of filling onto the base then cover with the remaining dough and bake. After baking leave to cool before cutting into fingers.

CHEQUERS

1. Beat the butter until soft and creamy, then beat in the sugar until light and fluffy.

2. Sift the flour into the creamed mixture and rub together to form a crumble texture. Divide the mixture into two equal portions then mix the drinking chocolate into one portion.

3. Continue mixing until crumbs bind together. Divide each portion into two and roll out to 20.5cm (8in) long. Wrap in foil and chill until firm.

4. When chilled cut each roll into four. Join alternate colours together using a little water. Cut into slices, place onto trays and bake.

INGREDIENTS
Makes 36

Metric		Imperial
145g	Butter or margarine	**5oz**
115g	Caster sugar	**4oz**
255g	Plain flour	**9oz**
7.5ml	Drinking chocolate	**1½tsp**

BAKING TRAYS

Well greased baking trays.

BAKING

Preheated oven, 180°C, 360°F
or gas mark 4
Middle shelf
8-10 minutes or until just firm

BROWNIES

INGREDIENTS
Makes 24

Metric		Imperial
115g	Butter or margarine	4oz
115g	Plain Scotbloc or Chocolat	4oz
115g	Dark brown soft sugar	4oz
115g	Self-raising flour	4oz
	Pinch of salt	
	2 eggs, size 3	
60g	Walnuts, chopped	2oz
15-30ml	Milk	1-2tbsp

TOPPING

115g	Milk or plain Scotbloc or Chocolat	4oz
60g	Unsalted butter	2oz
	1 egg, size 3	
170g	Icing sugar, sifted	6oz

BAKING TIN

Greased and lined with greaseproof paper 18 x 28cm (7 x 11in) shallow baking tin.

BAKING

Preheated oven, 180°C, 360°F or gas mark 4
Middle shelf
30-40 minutes

Mary's Tips

A soft dropping consistency is when the mixture just drops off the spoon.

If using a fan oven, the baking temperature may need adjusting.

This rich, moist traybake will store very well uncut in an airtight tin.

If you are watching the calories, this traybake is equally good without the topping.

1. *Place the butter and chocolate together in a bowl over a saucepan of hot water and leave until melted. Remove from the heat and stir in the sugar. Leave to cool.*

2. *Sift the flour with the salt into a mixing bowl. Make a well in the centre and pour in the cooled chocolate mixture. Mix together well.*

3. *Beat in the eggs and walnuts. Stir in sufficient milk to give a soft dropping consistency. Spread the mixture evenly in the tin and bake. Leave to cool in the tin.*

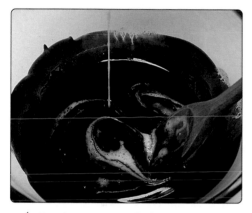

4. *For the topping, melt the chocolate and butter in a pan over hot water, stirring occasionally.*

5. *Thoroughly beat the egg and stir into the chocolate. Remove from the heat and stir in the icing sugar. Then beat well.*

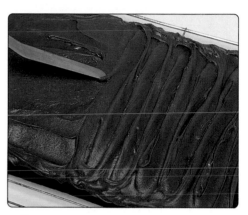

6. *Leave to cool slightly until the mixture thickens. Place the base onto a wire tray then spread the mixture with a palette knife over the top. Cut into squares.*

MELTING CHOCOLATE

This method should be used to melt chocolate flavoured coatings such as Scotbloc or Chocolat.

Melt the chocolate slowly on a very low heat, stirring gently. Stand the bowl over a saucepan which is small enough to support it without the bowl touching the base. The water level should not be allowed to touch the bowl and the water should simmer, not boil. Never try to hurry the melting process by turning up the heat. When the chocolate is almost melted, remove from the heat and continue stirring until the chocolate is smooth and completely melted. Keep it warm, stirring occasionally, to prevent it from setting while in use.

To melt Scotbloc in a microwave:

Place 225g (8oz) of broken plain Scotbloc in a non-metallic bowl. Microwave for 4-5 minutes on a medium setting, stirring once. When just softened, remove from the microwave and stir well until the chocolate has completely melted. It is important not to overheat beyond the point where the chocolate is just soft, as this makes it grainy and unmanageable. Milk Scotbloc will need slightly less time.

WHISKY SNAPS

1. Melt the syrup, sugar and butter together gently in a saucepan. Stir in the whisky. Sift the flour and ground ginger together.

2. Mix all the ingredients together until well blended. Drop teaspoonfuls onto the trays about 15cm (6in) apart and bake.

INGREDIENTS
Makes 36

Metric		Imperial
115g	Lyle's golden syrup	4oz
115g	Light brown soft sugar	4oz
115g	Butter	4oz
5ml	Whisky	1tsp
115g	Plain flour	4oz
10ml	Ground ginger	2tsp

FILLING

285g	Whipping cream	10oz

BAKING TRAYS

Well greased baking trays.

BAKING

Preheated oven, 180°C, 360°F
or gas mark 4
Middle shelf
Approximately 10 minutes or until
golden brown

Mary's Tips

Roll the snaps around the handles
as soon as possible before they
harden. If too cool then return to
oven to soften.

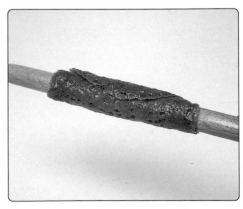

3. Immediately after baking leave to cool for a few seconds before rolling round the greased handle of a large wooden spoon. Slide off and fill with whipped cream when cold.

STICKLEBACKS

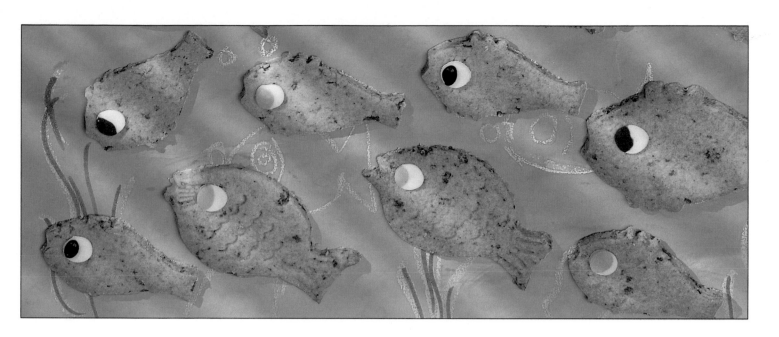

INGREDIENTS

Metric		Imperial
85g	Plain flour	3oz
85g	Self-raising flour	3oz
115g	Butter	4oz
60g	Light brown soft sugar	2oz
30g	Bran flakes, crushed finely	1oz

DECORATION

A little piece of sugarpaste or royal icing for the fish eyes

BAKING TRAYS

Well greased baking trays.

BAKING

Preheated oven, 180°C, 360°F or gas mark 4
Middle shelf
Approximately 20 minutes or until golden brown

Mary's Tips

Place equal sized fish on each tray to keep even colour when baking.

1. Sift the flours into a bowl then rub in the butter and sugar to give a breadcrumb mixture. Then add in the bran flakes.

2. Knead together to form a smooth, well mixed dough.

3. Roll the mixture on a lightly floured surface, cut out the fish and place onto trays and bake.

PEANUT CHEWS

INGREDIENTS
Makes 36

Metric		Imperial
115g	Butter	4oz
85g	Low fat soft cheese	3oz
2.5ml	Vanilla essence	½tsp
170g	Caster sugar	6oz
225g	Plain flour	8oz
	Pinch of salt	
115g	Peanuts, finely chopped	4oz

BAKING TRAYS

Well greased baking trays.

BAKING

Preheated oven, 190°C, 375°F
or gas mark 5
Middle shelf
Approximately 12 minutes or until
golden brown around the edges

Mary's Tips

Walnuts, finely chopped, can be substituted for peanuts.
This will give a stronger flavour.

1. Blend the butter, soft cheese and essence together. Gradually beat in the sugar until light and creamy.

2. Sift the flour and salt together into the mixture, add the chopped peanuts and blend to a soft dough.

3. Mould the dough into a roll and cut into 36 pieces. Mould into rounds, place onto trays and flatten slightly before marking with a fork. After baking leave on wire tray to cool.

LEMON FINGERS

1. Place all the ingredients in a mixing bowl and beat for three minutes on medium speed or for 5 minutes by hand with a wooden spoon.

2. Spread the mixture evenly into the prepared tin and bake. After baking place on a wire tray, remove the paper and leave until cold.

3. Mix the topping ingredients together to form a smooth, not too soft, icing. Spread over the sponge and leave to set before cutting. Decorate as required.

INGREDIENTS
Makes 30

Metric		Imperial
145g	Soft tub margarine	5oz
145g	Caster sugar	5oz
	Grated rind of 1 lemon	
	3 eggs, size 3	
145g	Self-raising flour	5oz
200g	Icing sugar, sifted	7oz
30ml	Lemon juice	2tbsp
	A little water	
	A few drops of yellow colouring	

DECORATION

Lemons made from sugarpaste or lemon slices

BAKING TIN

Greased and lined with greaseproof paper18 x 28cm (7 x 11in) shallow baking tin.

BAKING

Preheated oven, 180°C, 360°F or gas mark 4
Middle shelf
30-35 minutes

Mary's Tips

The grated rind and juice of orange or lime can be used to vary the flavour.

Decorate with sugarpaste, limes or oranges.

GINGERBREAD BISCUITS

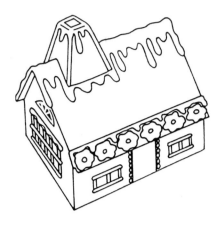

Increase the size of templates to that required.

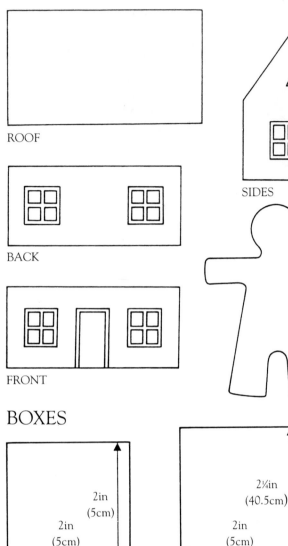

ROOF

BACK

FRONT

BOXES

2in (5cm)
2in (5cm)

2¼in (40.5cm)
2in (5cm)

2½in (45cm)
2¼in (40.5cm)

SIDES

CHIMNEY

1. Whisk the cream until it thickens slightly. Stir in the brown sugar, treacle, ginger, lemon rind and bicarbonate of soda and mix well together.

2. Immediately sift the flour into the mixture and gradually stir in.

3. Continue working in the flour until a smooth, pliable dough is formed. Roll out on lightly floured surface and cut the pieces required using the templates as a guide.

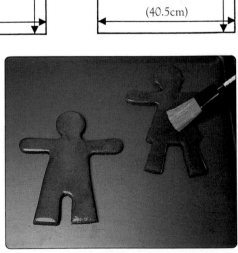

4. Carefully place onto the trays, without distorting the shapes then brush with water and bake. Remove from the trays to cool. Then fix boxes and decorate with royal icing.

INGREDIENTS

Metric		Imperial
170ml	Double cream	**6floz**
225g	Light brown soft sugar	**8oz**
225g	Lyle's black treacle	**8oz**
10ml	Ground ginger	**2tsp**
	Grated rind of 1 lemon	
10ml	Bicarbonate of soda	**2tsp**
570g	Plain flour	**20oz**

DECORATION

Royal icing
Variety of sweets

BAKING TRAYS

Well greased baking trays.

BAKING

Approximately 20-25 minutes, depending on thickness of biscuit

Preheated oven, 180°C, 360°F or gas mark 4
Middle shelf

Mary's Tips

This recipe is ideal for any cut-out shapes. Use the templates for a Gingerbread house to make an attractive centrepiece for a Christmas party.

To make the boxes, use the templates to cut out base and sides. Use a contrasting colour royal icing to secure pieces and then overpipe edges to neaten.

The eyes on the figure can be indented before baking.

Use Tate & Lyle traditional royal icing for quickness.

ALMOND MACAROONS

1. Mix the caster sugar, ground almonds and rice flour together in a bowl. Lightly whisk the egg whites.

2. Add sufficient beaten egg whites to the dry ingredients to form a stiff dough. Mould the dough to a long roll and cut into 16 pieces. Mould each piece into a ball.

INGREDIENTS

Makes 16

Metric		Imperial
170g	Caster sugar	6oz
115g	Ground almonds	4oz
5ml	Rice flour	1tsp
	1-2 egg whites	

DECORATION

Caster sugar for sprinkling
Split almonds

BAKING TRAYS

Well greased baking trays.

BAKING

Preheated oven, 180°C, 360°F
or gas mark 4
Middle shelf
Approximately 15 minutes or until
light brown

Mary's Tips

For variety: Omit the almonds and dip half the biscuit into melted chocolate when cool.

Always use eggs at room temperature for baking.

3. Place onto trays, allowing plenty of room for spreading during baking. Brush with remaining egg white, add a split almond then sprinkle with a little caster sugar and bake.

BANANA BREAKFAST SNACKS

Mary's Tips

These snacks freeze well.

Wrap in foil or place in a plastic container.

Will keep for up to two months.

1. Sift the flour and baking powder together into a mixing bowl. Stir in the muesli and sunflower seeds.

INGREDIENTS

Makes 16

Metric		Imperial
225g	Wholemeal self-raising flour	8oz
10ml	Baking powder	2tsp
145g	Unsweetened muesli	5oz
45g	Sunflower seeds	1½oz
170g	Butter	6oz
170g	Light brown soft sugar	6oz
	4 bananas	
	Juice of 1 lemon	
15ml	Sesame seeds	1tbsp

BAKING TIN

Lightly greased and lined with greaseproof paper 18 x 28cm (7 x 11in) shallow baking tin.

BAKING

Preheated oven, 180°C, 360°F or gas mark 4
Middle shelf
Approximately 40 minutes

2. Gently melt the butter in a saucepan then add the sugar and heat for a further 1-2 minutes. Mix thoroughly into the dry ingredients.

3. Spread two thirds into the prepared tin evenly. Peel and slice the bananas and toss in lemon juice then scatter into the tin.

4. Spoon the remaining mixture on top. Evenly sprinkle with sesame seeds and bake. Leave to cool in the tin then cut into squares.

SAVOURY WHIRLS

INGREDIENTS

Makes 15-20

Metric		Imperial
115g	Margarine	4oz
5ml	Light brown soft sugar	1tsp
145g	Plain flour	5oz
	Large pinch each of salt, pepper and paprika	
15ml	Sesame seeds	1tbsp
30ml	Parmesan cheese, grated	2tbsp
	Little milk (optional)	

DECORATION

Parmesan cheese, grated
Walnut pieces

BAKING TRAYS

Well greased baking trays.

BAKING

Preheated oven, 190°C, 375°F
or gas mark 5
Middle shelf
Approximately 15 minutes

1. Cream the margarine and sugar until soft. Sift the flour, salt, pepper and paprika together then mix in the sesame seeds and grated cheese.

2. Gradually work the dry ingredients into the creamed margarine to form a medium, soft dough. Mix in a few drops of milk if too stiff.

3. Fill a savoy bag, and star tube, with the mixture and pipe rosettes onto the prepared tins. Sprinkle with grated cheese then place walnut pieces on top and bake.

ALMOND CRUNCH FINGERS

1. Place the flour into a bowl and rub in the butter. Then mix in sufficient water to make a smooth pastry. Line the tin and crimp the edge with a fork. Spread with jam.

2. Warm the syrup, margarine and sugar together gently in a saucepan until the margarine has melted. Stir in the oats and essence to taste.

INGREDIENTS

Makes 20

Metric		Imperial
170g	Plain flour, sifted	6oz
85g	Butter	3oz
	Water to mix	
	Apricot jam	
85g	Lyle's golden syrup	3oz
85g	Margarine	3oz
30g	Light brown soft sugar	1oz
115g	Rolled oats	4oz
	Almond essence	

BAKING TIN

Well greased 18 x 28cm (7 x 11in) shallow baking tin.

BAKING

Preheated oven, 190°C, 375°F or gas mark 5
Middle shelf
Approximately 25 minutes or until golden brown

Mary's Tips

Flaked almonds can be added to the top of the mixture before baking.

3. Spoon the mixture over the jam and spread evenly with a spatula. After baking leave to cool then cut into fingers.

MARTINA'S LEBKUCHEN

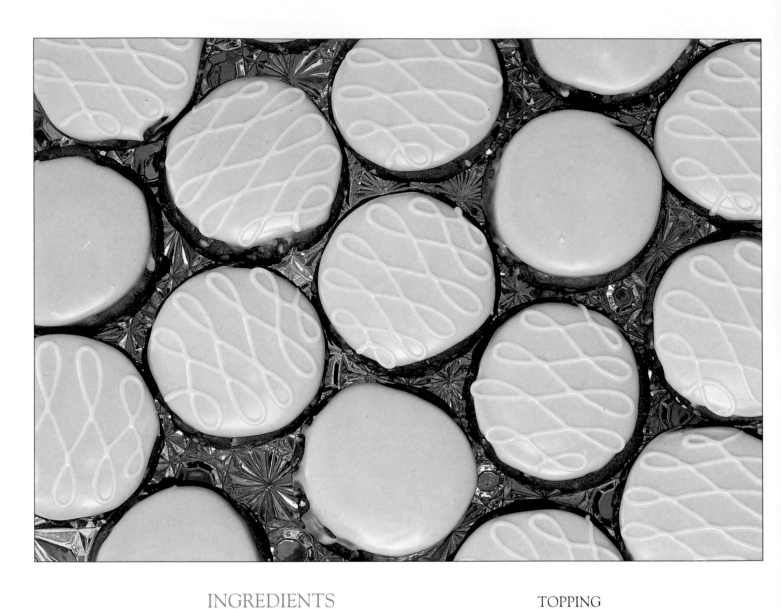

INGREDIENTS

Makes 30

Metric		Imperial
170g	Lyle's golden syrup	6oz
60g	Caster sugar	2oz
60g	Butter or margarine	2oz
30ml	Water	2tbsp
	1 egg yolk	
	Grated rind of ½ lemon	
15ml	Cocoa powder	1tbsp
5ml	Cinnamon	1tsp
	Pinch of ground nutmeg	
	Pinch of ground cardamon	
255g	Plain flour	9oz
145g	Almonds, finely chopped	5oz
60g	Mixed peel, chopped	2oz
60g	Raisins, chopped	2oz
15ml	Baking powder	3tsp

TOPPING

115g	Icing sugar, sifted	4oz
	1 egg white, lightly beaten	
	Few drops of lemon juice	
	Choice of food colours	

BAKING TRAYS

Well greased baking trays.

BAKING

Preheated oven, 180°C, 360°F
or gas mark 4
Middle shelf
20-25 minutes

1. Melt the syrup, sugar, butter and water in a bowl over low heat. Leave until cool.

2. Mix in the egg yolk and grated rind. Sift the cocoa powder and spices together with 170g (6oz) of the flour and beat into the mixture.

3. Thoroughly beat in the chopped almonds, peel and raisins.

Mary's Tips

It is important to thoroughly sift the dry ingredients three times.

A coating consistency runs off the spoon easily.

Cover the biscuits with water icing or for a more professional finish, use royal icing. Royal icing should always be used for piping.

4. Sift the remaining flour together with the baking powder and fold into the mixture. Gently knead on floured surface until well blended. Roll out to 6mm (¼in) thick.

5. Cut into rounds and bake. Beat the topping ingredients together to form a coating consistency. When biscuits are cold cover with the topping and decorate with piping.

WATER ICING

Metric		Imperial
15ml	Boiling water	**1tbsp**
60ml	Icing sugar, sifted	**4tbsp**
	Colour and flavouring to taste	

Place water into a bowl. Gradually stir in enough icing sugar to make a smooth paste which will coat and slowly drop off the back of a spoon.

ROYAL ICING

Metric		Imperial
115g	Icing sugar	**4oz**
	1 egg white, lightly beaten	
	Few drops of lemon juice	
	Choice of food colours	

Sift icing sugar into a bowl. Beat in egg white and continue beating until soft peak consistency. Add a few drops of glycerine for a softer eating icing.

GIGI'S CINNAMON STARS

INGREDIENTS

Makes 30

Metric		Imperial
	3 egg whites, size 3	
255g	Caster sugar	**9oz**
315g	Ground almonds	**11oz**
15ml	Ground cinnamon	**1tbsp**
	Icing sugar for dusting	

BAKING TRAYS

Bake on trays lined with parchment or rice paper.

BAKING

Preheated oven, 160°C, 320°F or gas mark 3
Middle shelf
20-25 minutes or until the meringue topping is golden brown

Mary's Tips

When making meringue, always sterilise the bowl and whisk with boiling water before use.

1. Whisk the egg whites until stiff and then fold in the caster sugar with a large spoon. Set aside 60ml (4tbsp) of the mixture for the topping.

2. Fold the ground almonds and cinnamon into the remaining mixture to form a dough.

3. Using icing sugar for dusting, roll out to 1cm (½in) thick then cut into star shapes and place onto prepared trays.

4. Spread a little of the meringue topping over each biscuit then bake until light golden brown.

DINOSAURUS

1. Mix together the butter, sugar, baking powder, juice and essence until light and fluffy.

2. Gradually stir in the flour until well mixed then knead to form a soft dough. Place in refrigerator for 2-3 hours until firm enough to roll out.

INGREDIENTS

Metric		Imperial
225g	Butter	8oz
170g	Caster sugar	6oz
	1 egg, size 3	
5ml	Baking powder	1tsp
30ml	Orange juice	2tbsp
5ml	Vanilla essence	1tsp
285g	Plain flour, sifted	10oz

DECORATION

Water icing (see page 27)
Plain or milk Scotbloc or Chocolat

BAKING TRAYS

Well greased baking trays.

BAKING

Preheated oven, 200°C, 400°F
or gas mark 6
Middle shelf
6-10 minutes or until edges are
lightly browned

Mary's Tips

Any shape cutter can be used.

These biscuits colour very quickly
so careful baking is essential.

3. Roll out the dough and cut around card shapes or with cutters. Place onto the trays and bake. Decorate with water icing and melted chocolate (see page 15).

MINCEMEAT SHORTBREAD

1. Cream the fat and sugar then gradually work in the sifted flour and mincemeat. Knead the mixture until well blended.

2. Roll out on a lightly floured surface then press evenly into the tin. Mark around the edge with a fork.

3. Press with a spoon to form pattern shown. Cut into 8 sections then prick all over and bake. After baking cut again, sprinkle with caster sugar then leave until cold.

INGREDIENTS
Makes 8

Metric		Imperial
115g	Margarine or butter	4oz
60g	Caster sugar	2oz
170g	Plain flour, sifted	6oz
60ml	Mincemeat	4tbsp

DECORATION

A little caster sugar

BAKING TIN

21.5cm (8½in) round sponge tin greased with margarine or butter.

BAKING

Preheated oven, 170°C, 340°F or gas mark 3
Middle shelf
25-30 minutes or until golden brown.

Mary's Tips

This is an excellent way of using up leftover mincemeat from Christmas.
Makes 8 or more pieces.

GINGER STARS

INGREDIENTS
Makes 18

Metric		Imperial
85g	Margarine	3oz
60g	Lyle's golden syrup	2oz
115g	Plain flour	4oz
6ml	Ground ginger	**1 rounded tsp**

DECORATION

Small pieces of glacé ginger

BAKING TRAYS

Well greased baking trays.

BAKING

Preheated oven, 170°C, 340°F
or gas mark 3
Middle shelf
12-15 minutes or until golden brown

Mary's Tips

These biscuits can also be piped thinly in fingers and sandwiched together with ginger jam or buttercream (see page 81).

1. Cream the margarine and syrup until blended. Sift the flour and ground ginger together and mix into the creamed mixture.

2. Place the mixture into a savoy bag, with a large star piping tube, and pipe stars on the greased trays. Top with glacé ginger and bake.

APPLE FLAPJACKS

INGREDIENTS
Makes 12

Metric		Imperial
115g	Butter	4oz
115g	Demerara sugar	4oz
45ml	Lyle's golden syrup	3tbsp
225g	Rolled oats	8oz
5ml	Ground cinnamon	1tsp
	1 cooking apple	

BAKING TIN

Well greased 18 x 28cm (7 x 11in) shallow baking tin.

BAKING

Preheated oven, 180°C, 360°F or gas mark 4
Middle shelf
Approximately 20 minutes or until flapjack is golden brown

Mary's Tips

A variety of ingredients can be added to the basic mixture.

Try chopped or flaked nuts, sesame seeds, dried fruit or chocolate drops.

1. Melt the butter, sugar and syrup in a saucepan over low heat until the butter has just melted.

2. Stir in the rolled oats and cinnamon. Peel the apple and dice the flesh finely.

3. Stir into the flapjack until well blended. Press the mixture evenly into the tin and bake. After baking allow to cool for 5 minutes then mark into bars. Cut when cold.

HAZELNUT COOKIES

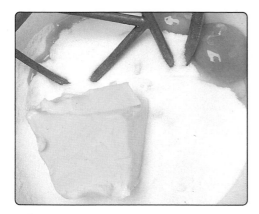

1. Place all the ingredients into a bowl and, using a beater on slow speed, blend together.

2. Remove from the bowl and gently knead together to form a smooth, firm dough. Leave to chill in the refrigerator for 1 hour.

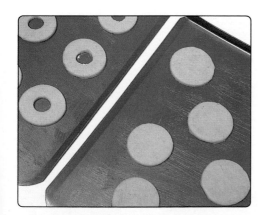

3. Roll out and cut into whole rounds and rings and then bake. When cold fix together with jam or preserve, dust with icing sugar and fill tops with piping jelly.

INGREDIENTS
Makes 30

Metric		Imperial
145g	Plain flour, sifted	5oz
145g	Butter	5oz
145g	Caster sugar	5oz
145g	Ground hazelnuts	5oz
	2 egg yolks	

DECORATION

Icing sugar for dusting
Jam or preserve
Piping jelly

BAKING TRAYS

Well greased baking trays.

BAKING

Preheated oven, 180°C, 360°F
or gas mark 4
Middle shelf
Approximately 15 minutes or until
golden brown

Mary's Tips

Piping jelly is available from most supermarkets.

Ensure ingredients are at room temperature before mixing.

NUT MERINGUE SLICES

INGREDIENTS
Makes 16

Metric		Imperial
60g	Light brown soft sugar	2oz
85g	Margarine	3oz
	2 egg yolks	
170g	Self-raising flour	6oz
5ml	Vanilla essence	1tsp

TOPPING

	2 egg whites	
85g	Caster sugar	3oz
30g	Walnuts, chopped	1oz
30g	Glacé cherries, chopped	1oz

BAKING TIN

Well greased 18 x 28cm (7 x 11in) shallow baking tin.

BAKING

Preheated oven, 180°C, 360°F
or gas mark 4
Middle shelf
20-25 minutes

Mary's Tips

For a good meringue always whisk the egg whites first until very stiff before adding the sugar. Use a sterilised, grease free bowl and whisk. Never use a wooden spoon for meringue.

Separating the eggs overnight helps the meringue to whisk stiffly.

1. Cream the brown sugar and margarine together. Gradually beat in the egg yolks.

2. Sift the flour and stir into the creamed mixture together with the essence to form pastry.

3. Roll the pastry on a lightly floured surface and gently press into the base of the tin.

4. Whisk the egg whites until stiff then add half the caster sugar. Whisk until very stiff.

5. Fold in the remaining sugar, chopped walnuts and cherries until evenly blended.

6. Spread the mixture over the pastry base to within 1cm (½in) of the edges and then bake. Cut into bars whilst still warm then leave in the tin until cold.

NO COOK TREATS

INGREDIENTS
Makes 28

Metric		Imperial
285g	Lyle's golden syrup	10oz
225g	Peanut butter	8oz
5ml	Vanilla essence	1tsp
225g	Cereal Bran	8oz
60g	Chopped peanuts	2oz

TOPPING

115g	Plain or milk Scotbloc or Chocolat	4oz

BAKING TIN

Well greased 18 x 28cm (7 x 11in) shallow baking tin.

1. Mix the syrup and peanut butter together in a large saucepan and cook over medium heat stirring until mixture begins to boil.

2. Remove from the heat and stir in the essence, bran cereal and chopped peanuts until well blended.

3. Spread the mixture into the prepared tin and lightly press out evenly. Chill for 1 hour.

4. Turn out onto greaseproof paper. Melt the chocolate (see page 15) and spread over the top using a palette knife or serrated scraper. Cut into squares when set.

ALMOND SHORTBREAD

1. Beat the butter until light and fluffy then thoroughly beat in the sugar.

2. Lightly fold in the flour, ground rice together with the nibbed or chopped almonds. Gently roll the mixture on a lightly floured surface.

3. Cut out circles, then place on trays. Press a flaked almond on top and bake. After baking sprinkle with caster sugar then leave to cool.

INGREDIENTS
Makes 24

Metric		Imperial
115g	Butter	4oz
60g	Caster sugar	2oz
115g	Plain flour, sifted	4oz
60g	Ground rice	2oz
30g	Nibbed or chopped almonds	1oz

DECORATION

Caster sugar
Flaked almonds

BAKING TRAY

Lightly greased baking trays.

BAKING

Preheated oven 190°C, 375°F
or gas mark 5
Middle shelf
10-15 minutes or until light brown

AUSTRIAN STREUSELS

1. *For the sponge cake combine the margarine, sugar, egg, milk and flour using a beater on slow speed.*

2. *For the filling mix the ingredients in a bowl to form a crumbly texture. Spread half the cake mixture into the tin then sprinkle half the filling on top.*

INGREDIENTS
Makes 16

Metric		Imperial
85g	Soft tub margarine	3oz
170g	Caster sugar	6oz
	1 egg, size 3	
100ml	Milk	3½fl oz
170g	Self-raising flour, sifted	6oz

FILLING

85g	Light brown soft sugar	3oz
30g	Self-raising flour, sifted	1oz
5ml	Cinnamon	1tsp
30g	Soft margarine, melted	1oz
60g	Walnuts, chopped	2oz

BAKING TIN

Well greased 20.5cm (8in) square baking tin.

BAKING

Preheated oven, 170°C, 340°F or gas mark 3
Middle shelf
35-40 minutes

Mary's Tips

Serve warm or cold with coffee.

3. *Spread remaining cake mixture on top then cover with the remaining filling and bake. Cut into squares when cold.*

CARAWAY COOKIES

Mary's Tips

Caraway seeds provide a contrasting texture and flavour.

INGREDIENTS
Makes 25-30

Metric		Imperial
85g	Margarine	3oz
30g	Light brown soft sugar	1oz
115g	Lyle's golden syrup	4oz
45g	Self-raising flour	1½oz
2.5ml	Ground ginger	½tsp
45g	Chopped peel	1½oz
15ml	Caraway seeds	1tbsp
225g	Medium oatmeal	8oz

BAKING TRAYS

Well greased baking trays.

BAKING

Preheated oven, 180°C, 360°F
or gas mark 4
Middle shelf
Approximately 20 minutes or until
golden in colour

1. Cream the margarine, sugar and syrup together.

2. Sift the flour and ground ginger together then place into the creamed mixture. Add the remaining ingredients and mix to a soft dough.

3. Roll out on a lightly floured surface to 6mm (¼in) thick, cut into 45mm (1¾in) diameter circles and bake. Leave to cool on wire trays.

ANISCOOKIES

INGREDIENTS
Makes 50

Metric		Imperial
255g	Plain flour	**9oz**
	4 egg whites, size 3	
255g	Caster sugar	**9oz**
7.5ml	Star anise	**½tbsp**
	Pinch of bicarbonate of soda	

BAKING TRAYS

Well greased baking trays.

BAKING

Preheated oven, 150°C, 300°F or gas mark 2

Middle shelf
Approximately 15-20 minutes

Mary's Tips

Star anise is the star shaped fruit of a tree native to China. It has a strong liquorice like flavour. Ground star anise is available from most large supermarkets. This is traditionally a hard biscuit.

1. Sift the flour into a bowl and leave in a warm place for 10 minutes. Whisk the egg whites until thick and then fold in the sugar.

2. Mix the anise and bicarbonate of soda into the flour. Fold gently into the whisked egg whites.

3. Fill a savoy bag and star tube with the mixture and pipe onto the baking trays. Leave to dry overnight in a warm kitchen and then bake.

EASTER BISCUITS

INGREDIENTS

Metric		Imperial
115g	Butter or margarine	4oz
115g	Caster sugar	4oz
	1 egg, size 3	
225g	Plain flour	8oz
5ml	Mixed spice	1tsp
60g	Currants	2oz
30g	Mixed peel	1oz

BAKING TRAYS

Well greased baking trays.

DECORATION

Milk or plain Scotbloc or Chocolat
Caster sugar
Royal icing

BAKING

Preheated oven, 180°C, 360°F
or gas mark 4
Middle shelf
15-20 minutes or until golden brown

Mary's Tips

Do not roll the mixture too thinly as the ears and beaks will brown quickly during baking. Sprinkle with caster sugar directly after baking if biscuits are not to be decorated.

1. Cream the fat and sugar until light, white and fluffy. Lightly beat the egg, then beat into the mixture a little at a time. Sift the flour and spice together.

2. Fold into the mixture. Stir in the dried fruits then knead until smooth. Place onto lightly floured surface. Roll out to 6mm (¼in) thick and cut shapes required.

3. Place even sized shapes onto trays, prick with a fork and bake. When cold, dip bases into melted chocolate and decorate as required.

BRAN SHORTIES

INGREDIENTS
Makes 32-40

Metric		Imperial
170g	Butter or margarine	6oz
225g	Light brown soft sugar	8oz
	1 egg, size 3	
225g	Self-raising flour, sifted	8oz
60g	Natural Bran	2oz

DECORATION

Icing sugar for dusting

BAKING TRAYS

Ungreased baking trays.

BAKING

Preheated oven, 220°C, 425°F or gas mark 7	Middle shelf 7-10 minutes or until golden brown

1. Cream the fat and sugar together until soft and creamy. Then thoroughly beat in the egg.

2. Lightly fold in the flour and bran until well mixed. Place onto a floured board and knead the mixture until smooth.

3. Divide in half and mould each into a roll 20.5cm (8in) long. Wrap in greaseproof paper or foil and chill until firm.

4. When chilled, cut each roll into 16 or 20 slices and bake. After baking place on cooling trays and dust with icing sugar.

CHOCOLATE CRACKLES

INGREDIENTS
Makes 20

Metric		Imperial
60g	Plain or milk Scotbloc or Chocolat	2oz
60g	Butter	2oz
60g	Lyle's golden syrup	2oz
60g	Caster sugar	2oz
45g	Rice Krispies	1½oz

1. Break the chocolate into small pieces. Melt the butter, syrup and sugar together over low heat then add the chocolate. Stir until melted but do not overheat.

2. Remove from heat then gently stir in the Rice Krispies until well blended. Place spoonfuls into paper cases and leave until set.

REDBERRY FRANGIPAN

INGREDIENTS
Makes 12

Metric		Imperial
145g	Plain flour	5oz
145g	Self-raising flour	5oz
85g	Caster sugar	3oz
145g	Butter, cubed	5oz
	1 egg, size 3	
15ml	Milk	1tbsp

FILLING

85g	Caster sugar	3oz
115g	Butter	4oz
	2 eggs, size 3	
115g	Ground almonds	4oz
60g	Seedless raspberry jam	2oz
60g	Frozen cranberries	2oz
60g	Frozen raspberries	2oz
	Milk for glaze	

DECORATION

A little caster sugar

BAKING TIN

30.5 x 10cm (12 x 4in) fluted rectangular flan tin.

BAKING

Preheated oven, 190°C, 375°F or gas mark 5
Middle shelf
20 minutes then 180°C, 360°F or gas mark 4 for a further 25-30 minutes

Mary's Tips

For added flavour, serve warm with cream and sprinkle with Demerara sugar.

This is ideal for a dessert.

1. Sift flours together into a large bowl. Stir in the sugar then rub in the butter until the mixture resembles fine breadcrumbs. Make a well in the centre and add the egg and milk.

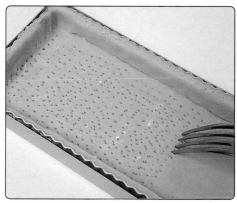

2. Knead until a soft smooth dough is made. Chill for 30 minutes then line the tin with the dough and prick with a fork. Reserve some dough for the trellis on top.

3. For the filling, cream the sugar and butter until light and fluffy. Gradually beat in the eggs and ground almonds.

4. Spread the raspberry jam over the base, using a palette knife.

5. Spread the filling over the jam and then sprinkle the frozen cranberries and raspberries on top.

6. Roll out the remaining dough and cut into narrow strips, fix in trellis pattern and glaze with milk and bake. Sprinkle with sugar and leave to cool in tin. Cut when cold.

CORNISH FAIRINGS

1. *Sift together the flour, salt, baking powder, spice, ginger and cinnamon into a bowl. Rub in the margarine until mixture resembles breadcrumbs, then stir in the sugar.*

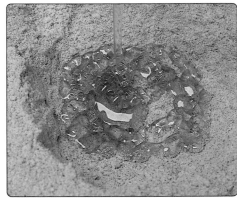

2. *Pour in the syrup and blend together to form a soft, smooth dough.*

INGREDIENTS
Makes 24

Metric		Imperial
225g	Plain flour	8oz
1.25ml	Salt	¼tsp
10ml	Baking powder	2tsp
10ml	Bicarbonate of soda	2tsp
10ml	Ground mixed spice	2tsp
15ml	Ground ginger	3tsp
5ml	Cinnamon	1tsp
115g	Margarine	4oz
115g	Caster sugar	4oz
170g	Lyle's golden syrup	6oz

BAKING TRAYS

Well greased baking trays.

BAKING

Preheated oven, 180°C, 360°F
or gas mark 4
Middle shelf
7 minutes or until golden brown

Mary's Tips

Careful baking is essential to
avoid over-colouring, especially
when using a fan oven.

3. *Roll the dough into walnut-sized pieces, place onto the trays and bake. Do not move the trays during baking as the biscuits may collapse too early.*

PEANUT TRIANGLES

INGREDIENTS
Makes 20

Metric		Imperial
115g	Butter	4oz
170g	Plain flour, sifted	6oz
60g	Light brown soft sugar	2oz
45g	Peanuts, finely chopped	1½oz

TOPPING

60g	Peanuts, roughly chopped	2oz
45g	Demerara sugar	1½oz

BAKING TIN

Lightly greased 20.5cm (8in) square, shallow baking tin.

BAKING

Preheated oven, 180°C, 360°F
or gas mark 4
Middle shelf
30-35 minutes or until golden brown

Mary's Tips

For variation, use chopped almonds instead of peanuts.

Optional topping: omit the peanuts and sugar. When cold, drizzle the tops with water icing, melted Scotbloc or Chocolat.

1. Rub the butter into the sifted flour until it resembles fine breadcrumbs. Stir in the sugar and peanuts.

2. Knead the mixture well until it binds together. Press evenly into the tin then prick with a fork.

3. Mix the peanuts and sugar together then sprinkle on top and bake. Leave to cool for 10 minutes after baking then cut into triangles and leave on a wire tray until cold.

CHOCOLATE CRUNCHIES

1. Sift the flour and salt together twice. Cream the fat and sugar in a separate mixing bowl. Beat in the egg.

2. Fold in the sifted flour and salt, then the chocolate pieces.

3. Mould the mixture into a long roll, divide into 24 pieces. Place onto the trays and press with a fork then bake. Leave on trays to cool.

INGREDIENTS
Makes 24

Metric		Imperial
170g	Plain flour	6oz
	Pinch of salt	
85g	Butter or margarine	3oz
115g	Demerara sugar	4oz
	1 egg, size 3	
85g	Plain Scotbloc or Chocolat cut into tiny pieces	3oz

BAKING TRAYS

Well greased baking trays.

BAKING

Preheated oven, 180°C, 360°F or gas mark 4
Middle shelf
10-15 minutes or until firm

Mary's Tips

This is a really hard crunchy biscuit. Store in an airtight container to keep crisp.

LEMON COOKIES

INGREDIENTS
Makes 24

Metric		Imperial
85g	Butter	3oz
60g	Caster sugar	2oz
15ml	Lyle's golden syrup	1tbsp
	Grated rind of 1 lemon	
	1 egg yolk	
115g	Plain flour	4oz
30g	Cornflour	1oz

DECORATION

Icing sugar for dusting
Lemon curd

BAKING TRAYS

Well greased baking trays.

BAKING

Preheated oven, 170°C, 340°F
or gas mark 3
Middle shelf
After 15 minutes of baking, press each
top with the handle of a wooden spoon
to form a well.
Continue baking for another 5 minutes
or until golden brown.

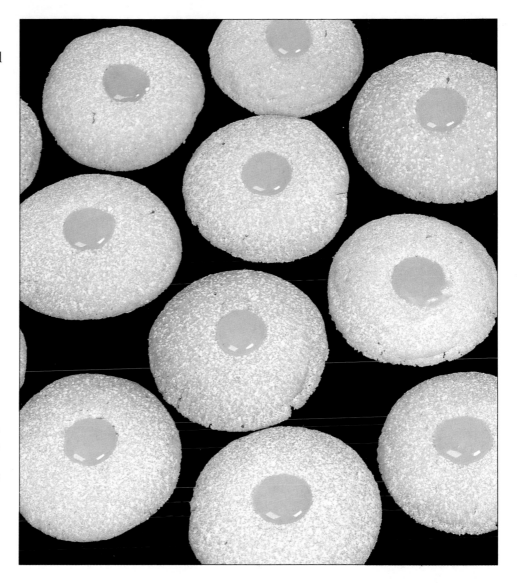

1. Cream the butter, sugar, syrup and rind together well with a wooden spoon. Thoroughly beat in the egg yolk. Sift the plain flour and cornflour together.

2. Using a spatula, gradually fold in the sifted flours to form a well blended dough. Mould the dough into a roll and cut into 24 pieces.

3. Roll each piece into a ball, place onto trays and bake (see baking instructions above). When cold, dust with icing sugar then fill tops with lemon curd.

SPICED RUM COOKIES

INGREDIENTS

Makes 30

Metric		Imperial
115g	Light brown soft sugar	4oz
	2 eggs, size 3, separated	
225g	Plain flour	8oz
5ml	Ground cinnamon	1tsp
	Pinch of ground ginger	
	Pinch of allspice	
	Pinch of ground cloves	
85g	Caster sugar	3oz
30g	Mixed peel	1oz
	Grated rind of 1 lemon	
60g	Ground almonds	2oz

DECORATION

Rum
Icing sugar for dusting

BAKING TRAYS

Well greased baking trays.

BAKING

Preheated oven, 190°C, 375°F
or gas mark 5
Middle shelf
10-15 minutes or until light brown

Mary's Tips

Brush the rum on while cookies are still hot.

These cookies improve with keeping. Store in an airtight tin.

1. Beat together the brown sugar with the egg yolks until light and fluffy. Sift the flour and spices together then stir in until the mixture resembles breadcrumbs.

2. Whisk the egg whites until they are stiff peaks and then beat in the caster sugar until glossy. Fold into the mixture with the peel and ground almonds. Leave covered overnight.

3. Roll the mixture into walnut size pieces, place onto the trays and bake. Brush with rum and sprinkle with icing sugar whilst still warm.

APPLE and DATE SHORTCAKE

1. Beat the fat and sugar until light and fluffy. Gradually beat in the egg a little at a time.

2. Sift the flour then stir into the mixture to form a well blended pastry. Roll out and place half the mixture into the tin.

3. Mix the apples and dates together and spread onto the pastry. Place remaining pastry on top and bake. When baked sprinkle with caster sugar and cut into bars when cold.

INGREDIENTS
Makes 12-16

Metric		Imperial
115g	Butter or margarine	4oz
85g	Caster sugar	3oz
	1 egg, size 3	
170g	Self-raising flour	6oz
225g	Cooking apples, cooked	8oz
115g	Dates, chopped	4oz

DECORATION

A little caster sugar for dusting

BAKING TIN

Lightly greased 18cm (7in) square shallow tin.

BAKING

Preheated oven, 180°C, 360°F or gas mark 4
Middle shelf
35-40 minutes

CHOCOLATE WALNUT BARS

Mary's Tips

For variation, try Lyle's black treacle as a substitute for golden syrup in the topping.

Then sprinkle with coconut.

INGREDIENTS
Makes 16

Metric		Imperial
85g	Margarine	3oz
115g	Plain flour	4oz
85g	Rolled oats	3oz
2.5ml	Baking powder	½tsp
115g	Demerara sugar	4oz

TOPPING

85g	Plain Scotbloc or Chocolat	3oz
85g	Milk Scotbloc or Chocolat	3oz
60g	Margarine	2oz
225g	Lyle's golden syrup	8oz
60g	Plain flour	2oz
5ml	Vanilla essence	1tsp
115g	Walnuts, chopped	4oz

DECORATION

60g	White Scotbloc, melted	2oz

BAKING TIN

Well greased 18 x 28cm (7 x 11in) shallow baking tin.

BAKING

Preheated oven, 180°C, 360°F or gas mark 4
Middle shelf
After 10 minutes add the topping then bake for a further 20-25 minutes

1. For the base, melt the margarine, remove from heat and stir in the flour, oats, baking powder and sugar. Mix well then spread evenly in the tin and bake for 10 minutes.

2. For the topping, melt the chocolate with the margarine and syrup. Remove from heat and stir in the flour, essence and walnuts.

3. After the base has been baking for 10 minutes, remove from oven and spread the topping mixture evenly over the base and return to the oven for 20-25 minutes.

4. Cool in the tin for 10 minutes, then loosen around the edges and cut into bars.

5. Place a wire tray over the tin, upturn and remove the tin. Place a second wire tray on the top, and upturn again.

6. Leave to cool on the tray then melt the white chocolate and drizzle in fine swirling lines. Separate the bars when the chocolate has set.

FINNISH GINGERS

INGREDIENTS
Makes 50

Metric		Imperial
85g	Margarine	3oz
60g	Caster sugar	2oz
115g	Lyle's golden syrup	4oz
200g	Self-raising flour	7oz
2.5ml	Ground cinnamon	½tsp
2.5ml	Ground ginger	½tsp
2.5ml	Ground cloves	½tsp
2.5ml	Bicarbonate of soda	½tsp
5ml	Water	1tsp

BAKING TRAYS

Lightly greased baking trays.

BAKING

Preheated oven, 150°C, 300°F
or gas mark 2
Middle shelf
10-15 minutes or until golden brown

Mary's Tips

Cut slices as thinly as possible
to make a crisper biscuit.
The thinner the biscuit the less
baking time required.

1. Melt the margarine, sugar and syrup over gentle heat. Sift the flour and spices then stir into the mixture.

2. Dissolve the bicarbonate of soda in the water and mix in to form a soft dough. Cover the bowl and leave overnight in a cool place.

3. Mould the dough into a small loaf shape about 20.5cm (8in) long. Cut into thin slices, place onto trays and bake.

COCONUT MUNCHIES

1. Cream the vegetable fat, margarine and sugar until light and fluffy. Gradually beat in the egg a little at a time.

2. Fold in the flour and half the coconut. Add the lemon juice and mix until well blended.

INGREDIENTS
Makes 24

Metric		Imperial
85g	Vegetable fat	3oz
30g	Margarine	1oz
85g	Caster sugar	3oz
	1 egg, size 3, beaten	
145g	Self-raising flour	5oz
60g	Desiccated coconut	2oz
10ml	Lemon juice	2tbsp

DECORATION

Glacé cherries, halved

BAKING TRAYS

Well greased baking trays.

BAKING

Preheated oven, 190°C, 375°F or gas mark 5
Middle shelf
10-12 minutes or until golden brown

Mary's Tips

Because vegetable fats and lard have less liquid they contain the most shortening power.

3. Mould the mixture into walnut sized pieces, then roll in the remaining coconut, place on the trays well apart. Top each with half a glacé cherry and bake.

MARBLED BARS

1. Blend the cocoa and hot water together and leave to cool. Place the remaining ingredients into a mixing bowl and beat for 2-3 minutes on medium speed.

2. Divide the mixture into two equal portions. Stir the cocoa mixture into one portion until well blended.

INGREDIENTS
Makes 16

Metric		Imperial
15ml	Cocoa powder	**1tbsp**
15ml	Boiling water	**1tbsp**
170g	Soft tub margarine	**6oz**
170g	Caster sugar	**6oz**
170g	Self-raising flour	**6oz**
7.5ml	Baking powder	**1½tsp**
	3 eggs, size 3	

BAKING TIN

Greased and fully lined with greaseproof paper 18 x 28cm (7 x 11in) shallow baking tin.

BAKING

Preheated oven, 170°C, 340°F or gas mark 3
Middle shelf
Approximately 25 minutes or when firm to the touch

Mary's Tips

When cooked this traybake should spring back when lightly pressed on the top, and have slightly shrunk from the sides of the tin.

3. Using a dessert spoon, place alternate spoonfuls of mixture into the tin and then bake. Leave to cool in the tin for 10 minutes then turn out onto a wire tray to cool.

EMPIRE BISCUITS

INGREDIENTS
Makes 24

Metric		Imperial
85g	Margarine	3oz
60g	Lyle's golden syrup	2oz
	1 egg yolk	
145g	Plain flour	5oz
30g	Cornflour	1oz
10ml	Cinnamon	2tsp

FILLING

Jam or preserve of choice

TOPPING

See page 27 for water icing

BAKING TRAYS

Well greased baking trays.

BAKING

Preheated oven, 180°C, 360°F
or gas mark 4
Middle shelf
Approximately 10 minutes or just
brown around the edges

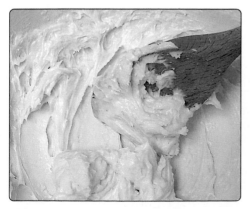

*1. Thoroughly cream the margarine,
syrup and egg yolk together.*

*2. Sift together the flour, cornflour and
cinnamon then blend into the creamed
mixture to form a smooth dough.*

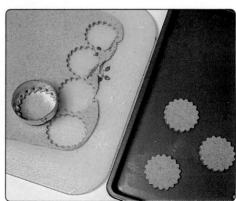

*3. Roll out thinly on a lightly floured
surface, cut out with a fluted cutter and
bake. When cold, sandwich together
with jam then coat the tops with
feathered water icing.*

CHEESE TRAYBAKE

INGREDIENTS
Makes 18

Metric		Imperial
285g	Light brown soft sugar	10oz
340g	Plain flour	12oz
170g	Butter, melted	6oz

FILLING

400g	Cream cheese	14oz
60g	Lyle's golden syrup	2oz
225g	Caster sugar	8oz
	2 eggs, size 3, beaten	
30ml	Lemon juice	2tbsp
60ml	Milk	4tbsp
5ml	Vanilla essence	1tsp

BAKING TIN

Well greased 18 x 28cm (7 x 11in) shallow baking tin.

BAKING

Preheated oven, 180°C, 360°F or gas mark 4
Middle shelf
20 minutes for the base, then 10 minutes with the filling and finally 20 minutes with the topping.

Mary's Tips

This cheese traybake also makes an ideal dessert, served hot or cold.

Can be served with strawberries or other fruits.

Be very careful when you remove from tin. It is best cooled completely in the tin first.

1. Combine the brown sugar and flour in a large bowl, stir in the melted butter until the mixture resembles breadcrumbs.

2. Fill the tin with two thirds of the mixture then press down evenly and firmly. Bake for 20 minutes.

3. Meanwhile beat the cream cheese, syrup and caster sugar until smooth.

4. Beat in the egg, lemon juice, milk and vanilla essence.

5. After the base has cooked, remove from the oven and leave for 2 minutes then pour on the creamed filling. Return to the oven for 10 minutes.

6. Then carefully remove and sprinkle on the remaining crumb mixture and bake for the last 20 minutes. Leave to cool in the tin, cut into fingers.

NUTTY WAFERS

1. Beat the margarine, sugar and syrup together until light and fluffy. Thoroughly beat in the egg and vanilla essence.

2. Sift the flour and bicarbonate of soda together, lightly stir into the mixture with the peanuts to form a soft dough.

3. Place walnut sized rounds onto the trays and bake. Leave on the tray for a few moments before cooling on wire trays.

INGREDIENTS
Makes 36

Metric		Imperial
115g	Margarine	4oz
60g	Caster sugar	2oz
170g	Lyle's golden syrup	6oz
	1 egg, size 3	
5ml	Vanilla essence	½tsp
145g	Plain flour	5oz
2.5ml	Bicarbonate of soda	¼tsp
85g	Roasted peanuts	3oz

BAKING TRAYS

Well greased trays or trays lined with parchment paper.

BAKING

Preheated oven, 180°C or 360°F or gas mark 4
Middle Shelf
Approximately 15 minutes or until golden brown.

Mary's Tips

Never warm syrup in a plastic bowl in a microwave as this may melt.

Good with ice cream.

VIENNESE SHELLS

1. *Using a wooden spoon, beat the fat and icing sugar until creamy.*

2. *Gradually work in the flour to form a soft dough. Place a star savoy tube into a piping bag and fill with the mixture.*

INGREDIENTS
Makes 30

Metric		Imperial
170g	Butter or margarine	6oz
60g	Icing sugar, sifted	2oz
170g	Plain flour, sifted	6oz

DECORATION

Glacé cherries, halved
Plain or milk Scotbloc or Chocolat, melted

BAKING TRAYS

Well greased baking trays.

BAKING

Preheated oven, 150°C, 300°F or gas mark 2
Middle shelf
20-30 minutes or until lightly brown

Mary's Tips

Viennese can be piped as shells, rosettes, fingers and stars.

3. *Pipe shells onto the trays. Place a half glacé cherry on some shells then bake. When cold dip some of the shells into melted chocolate (see page 15).*

WHOLEWHEAT CRUNCHIES

1. Place the dry ingredients in a bowl, add butter cut into small pieces and rub in until breadcrumb consistency.

2. Add the egg and mix with a fork until the mixture holds together. Place onto a floured surface and knead until smooth. Cover and leave for 10 minutes.

3. Roll out to the required size. Place onto the tray and cut into sections then bake.

INGREDIENTS
Makes 8

Metric		Imperial
145g	Wholewheat flour	5oz
1.25ml	Salt	¼tsp
2.5ml	Baking powder	½tsp
30g	Caster sugar	1oz
85g	Butter	3oz
	1 egg, size 4	

BAKING TRAY

Baking tray lightly dusted with flour.

BAKING

Preheated oven, 180°C, 360°F
or gas mark 4
Middle shelf
10-15 minutes or until golden brown

GINGER TOPPED SHORTCAKE

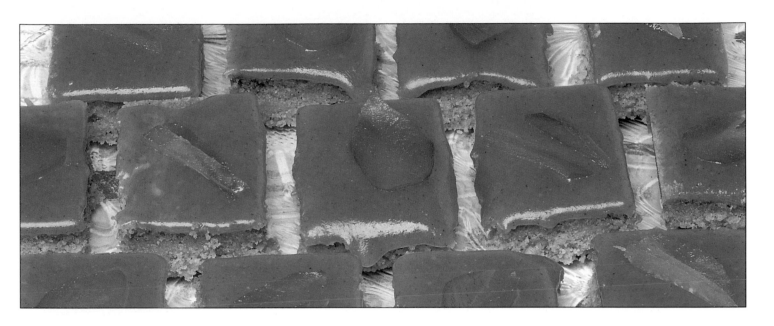

INGREDIENTS
Makes 16

Metric		Imperial
115g	Margarine	4oz
60g	Caster sugar	2oz
145g	Plain flour	5oz
10ml	Ground ginger	2tsp

TOPPING

60ml	Icing sugar, sifted	4tbsp
10ml	Ground ginger	2tsp
30g	Lyle's golden syrup	1oz
60g	Margarine	2oz

BAKING TIN

Well greased 20.5cm (8in) square shallow tin.

BAKING

Preheated oven, 170°C, 340°F
or gas mark 3
Middle shelf
25-30 minutes or until golden brown

Mary's Tips
Do not boil the topping too much.
Pour the topping on quickly.
Decorate with pieces of preserved ginger for extra bite.

1. Cream the margarine and sugar together until light and fluffy. Sift the flour and ginger together then stir into the mixture. Knead together to form a smooth, firm dough.

2. Roll out and fit evenly into the base of the tin and bake. Leave to cool after baking. For the topping, place all the ingredients into a saucepan and bring to the boil.

3. Leave to cool slightly then spread evenly over the shortcake. Leave to set in a cold place before removing from the tin and cutting.

CINNAMON BISCUITS

INGREDIENTS
Makes 20

Metric		Imperial
170g	Plain flour, sifted	6oz
2.5ml	Ground cinnamon	½tsp
115g	Unsalted butter	4oz
60g	Caster sugar	2oz
	1 egg, size 4, beaten	

TOPPING

15ml	Granulated sugar	1tbsp
2.5ml	Ground cinnamon	½tsp
30g	Flaked almonds	1oz

BAKING TIN

Well greased 18 x 28cm (7 x 11in)
shallow baking tin.

BAKING

Preheated oven, 170°C, 340°F
or gas mark 3
Middle shelf
Approximately 15 minutes or until
golden brown

*1. Sift the flour and cinnamon together
into a large bowl. Rub in the butter until
the mixture resembles fine breadcrumbs,
stir in the sugar.*

*2. Place the mixture into the tin and
press to form an even base. Brush with
the beaten egg.*

*3. Mix the topping ingredients together
then sprinkle onto the base and bake. Cut
into shapes whilst still warm.*

ICED and SPICED TREATS

1. Cut the butter into pieces and place in a large bowl. Place the sugar, treacle and spices into a saucepan and bring to boil. Add the bicarbonate of soda and pour into the bowl.

2. Stir until the butter has melted then beat in the egg. Stir in the flour. Knead the mixture to form a smooth manageable dough.

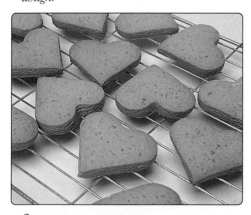

3. Roll out on lightly floured surface to 6mm (¼in) thickness. Cut into heart shapes, place onto trays and bake. Using recipe on page 27, decorate as required when cold.

INGREDIENTS
Makes 50

Metric		Imperial
115g	Butter	4oz
100g	Demerara sugar	3½oz
200g	Lyle's black treacle	7oz
5ml	Ground ginger	1tsp
5ml	Ground cinnamon	1tsp
2.5ml	Ground cloves	½tsp
5ml	Bicarbonate of soda	1tsp
	1 egg, size 3	
510g	Plain flour, sifted	1lb2oz

DECORATION

1 Egg white
Icing sugar (see page 27)
Various food colours
Nuts, finely chopped

BAKING TRAYS

Well greased baking trays.

BAKING

Preheated oven, 170°C, 340°F
or gas mark 3
Middle shelf
Approximately 10-15 minutes or until golden brown

Mary's Tips
Any shaped cutter can be used.
Use royal icing to add names for a party.

APPLE SULTANA TRAYBAKE

INGREDIENTS
Makes 12

Metric		Imperial
255g	Self-raising flour	9oz
	Pinch of salt	
30ml	Cornflour	2tbsp
2.5ml	Ground cloves	½tsp
85g	Margarine	3oz
5ml	Grated lemon rind	1tsp
70g	Light brown soft sugar	2½oz
	1 egg yolk	
90ml	Milk	6tbsp

FILLING

570g	Cooking apples, peeled, cored and sliced	1¼lb
15ml	Lemon juice	1tbsp
30ml	Water	2tbsp
5ml	Grated lemon rind	1tsp
60g	Sultanas	2oz
30ml	Lyle's golden syrup	2tbsp

DECORATION

Icing sugar for dusting

BAKING TIN

Lightly greased 18 x 28cm (7 x 11in) shallow baking tin.

BAKING

Preheated oven, 220°C, 425°F or gas mark 7
Middle shelf
Bake for 10 minutes then reduce heat to 190°C, 375°F or gas mark 5 and bake for further 20 minutes or until golden brown and the pastry is cooked through.

1. Sift the flour, salt, cornflour and ground cloves into a bowl. Rub in the margarine until the mixture resembles fine breadcrumbs.

2. Stir in the lemon rind and sugar, then bind to a pliable dough with the egg yolk and milk.

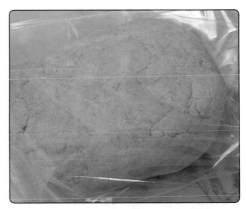

3. Knead on a lightly floured surface until smooth, then wrap in polythene and chill whilst making the filling.

4. Place the sliced apples, lemon juice and water in a pan and cook gently until just tender. Remove from the heat, stir in the lemon rind, fruit and syrup then leave until cold.

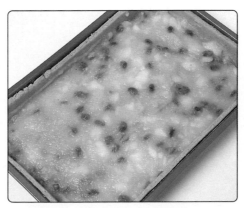

5. Roll out two thirds of the dough and line the tin. Spread the filling evenly over the pastry. Roll out the remaining dough and cut into narrow strips.

6. Twist the strips as shown, using a little dab of water to fix, and then bake. After baking dust with icing sugar then leave to cool in the tin before cutting into slices.

CHEESE BISCUITS

INGREDIENTS
Makes 14

Metric		Imperial
100g	Matured Cheddar cheese	3½oz
60g	Ready salted potato crisps	2oz
70g	Plain flour	2½oz
5ml	Icing sugar	1tsp
4ml	Mustard powder	¾tsp
	Pinch of cayenne pepper	
70g	Butter	2½oz

BAKING TRAYS

Well greased baking trays.

BAKING

Preheated oven, 190°C, 375°F
or gas mark 5
Middle shelf
Approximately 15 minutes or until
golden brown

Mary's Tips

Use a strong flavoured cheese
for maximum flavour.

1. Grate the cheese into a bowl. Crush the crisps lightly and mix in. Sift together the flour, icing sugar, mustard powder and cayenne pepper and stir into the mixture.

2. Melt the butter and stir into the mixture until well blended.

3. Divide the mixture into 14 pieces and place onto the trays in small heaps and bake. Leave to cool on the trays for 3-4 minutes then cool on a wire tray.

APRICOT FRUIT FINGERS

INGREDIENTS
Makes 24

Metric		Imperial
170g	Plain wholemeal flour	6oz
115g	Plain flour, sifted	4oz
5ml	Ground cinnamon	1tsp
170g	Soft tub margarine	6oz
30ml	Lyle's golden syrup	2tbsp
170g	No-need to soak apricots, chopped	6oz
85g	Mixed nuts, chopped	3oz
60g	Glacé cherries, chopped	3oz
	1 egg, size 3, beaten	
115ml	Unsweetened orange juice	4floz

BAKING TIN

Well greased 18 x 28cm (7 x 11in) shallow baking tin.

BAKING

Preheated oven, 190°C, 375°F or gas mark 5
Middle shelf
Bake the base for 20 minutes, add the topping, then bake for a further 15 minutes or until topping is set but still soft.

1. Place 115g (4oz) of wholemeal flour with the plain flour and cinnamon into a bowl. Mix in the margarine and syrup.

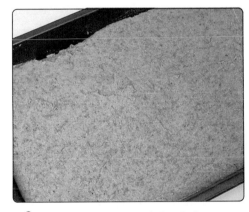

2. Mix well to form a soft dough then roll out and fit evenly into the tin and bake for 20 minutes.

3. Meanwhile make the topping. Mix together the remaining wholemeal flour, chopped fruits and nuts until well blended. Then stir in the egg and orange juice.

4. Remove the biscuit base from the oven after 20 minutes then spread on the topping evenly and bake for another 15 minutes. Leave to cool in the tin then cut into bars.

MELTING MOMENTS

1. Cream the butter and sugar until light and fluffy. Then gradually beat in the egg.

2. Gently fold in the sifted flour. Roll the mixture on floured surface and divide into 16 pieces.

INGREDIENTS
Makes 16

Metric		Imperial
60g	Butter	2oz
60g	Caster sugar	2oz
	1 egg, size 3	
115g	Self-raising flour, sifted	4oz

DECORATION

Rolled oats
Coloured glacé cherries

BAKING TRAYS

Well greased baking trays.

BAKING

Preheated oven, 180°C or 360°F or gas mark 4
Middle Shelf
15-20 minutes or until golden brown

3. Mould each piece into a ball then roll in the oats to cover. Place onto the trays, flatten slightly then bake. After baking place half a cherry on each biscuit then leave until cold.

Mary's Tips

Allow the eggs to stand out of the refrigerator overnight to reach room temperature before using.

Place well apart on the trays.

KATIES KRUNCH

1. *Crush the biscuits into a bowl. Sift in the icing sugar and coconut. Mix well. Melt chocolate (see page 15). Stir in the butter and add to the crumbled biscuits.*

2. *Spread the mixture into the tin and chill for a few minutes. Melt the white chocolate over hot water then spread evenly over the top.*

INGREDIENTS
Makes 28

Metric		Imperial
115g	Wheatmeal biscuits	4oz
60g	Icing sugar	2oz
30g	Desiccated coconut	1oz
145g	Plain Scotbloc or Chocolat	5oz
115g	Butter	4oz

TOPPING

115g	White Scotbloc	4oz

DECORATION

A little toasted desiccated coconut

BAKING TIN

Lightly greased 20.5cm (8in) square shallow baking tin.

Mary's Tips

Remember to chill the mixture for just a few moments before adding the topping as the chocolate may separate when cut.

3. *Immediately sprinkle with toasted coconut. Leave in the refrigerator for 1 hour. Turn out and cut into fingers.*

GOLDEN EYES

INGREDIENTS
Makes 24

Metric		Imperial
115g	Butter	4oz
60g	Caster sugar	2oz
30g	Lyle's golden syrup	1oz
	1 egg, size 3, separated	
145g	Plain flour, sifted	5oz

DECORATION

115g	Chopped nuts	4oz
	Apricot Pureé	

BAKING TRAYS

Well greased baking trays.

BAKING

Preheated oven, 170°C, 340°F
or gas mark 3
Middle shelf

15-20 minutes, pressing in the centres
again after the first 5 minutes of baking

Mary's Tips

Apricot jam can be used for the centres if pushed through a sieve to achieve a smooth, clear texture.

Alternatively, seedless raspberry jam can be used.

Chopped almonds or peanuts can be used instead of chopped nuts.

1. Place the butter, sugar, syrup and egg yolk into a bowl and cream together.

2. Stir in the sifted flour to form a smooth dough. Chill in refrigerator until firm.

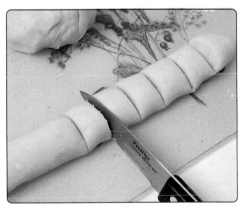

3. When chilled, divide the mixture in two, roll out and then cut each length into 12 pieces. Then roll into balls. Beat the egg white lightly in a small bowl.

4. Place the chopped nuts into another bowl. Dip three balls at a time into the egg white then roll in the nuts, using a fork.

5. Place onto greased trays then indent the tops with the handle of a wooden spoon.

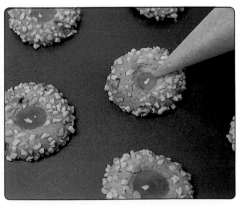

6. Bake in the oven for five minutes then press the tops again. Continue baking until golden brown. When cold, pipe apricot pureé into the centres.

FLAPJACKS

INGREDIENTS

Makes 12

Metric		Imperial
170g	Rolled oats	6oz
115g	Light brown soft sugar	4oz
85g	Butter or margarine	3oz
60g	Lyle's golden syrup	2oz

DECORATION

A little plain or milk Scotbloc or Chocolat, melted

BAKING TIN

Well greased 28 x 18cm (11 x 7in) shallow baking tin.

BAKING

Preheated oven, 180°C, 360°F
or gas mark 4
Middle shelf
20minutes or until golden brown

Mary's Tips

It s very important to grease the tin well for this recipe.

Flapjacks can be dipped in melted chocolate.

1. Mix the oats and sugar together in a bowl, melt the butter and syrup together in a saucepan.

2. Mix the dry ingredients into the saucepan until well blended then spoon into the greased tin.

3. Press the mixture evenly into the tin then bake. After baking leave to cool slightly then cut into fingers or bars. Turn out when cold.

CHERRY PEEL BARS

1. Whisk the egg and sugar until foamy then beat in the syrup. Fold in the melted butter, essence, peel, almonds and cherries. Then carefully fold in the flour until well blended.

2. Pour the mixture into the greased tin and level out then bake in the preheated oven until golden brown.

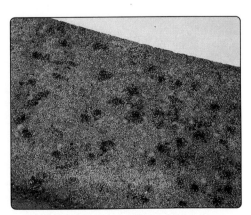

3. After baking, cool slightly then turn out onto greaseproof paper sprinkled with caster sugar. Sprinkle the top with more caster sugar. When cold cut into fingers as required.

INGREDIENTS
Makes 20

Metric		Imperial
	2 eggs, size 3	
115g	Light brown soft sugar	4oz
115g	Lyle's golden syrup	4oz
30ml	Butter, melted	2tbsp
2.5ml	Vanilla essence	½tsp
30g	Candied peel, chopped	1oz
30g	Blanched almonds, chopped	1oz
60g	Glacé cherries, quartered	2oz
115g	Self-raising flour, sifted	4oz

BAKING TIN

Well greased 18 x 28cm (7 x 11in) shallow baking tin.

BAKING

Preheated oven, 180°C, 360°F or gas mark 4
Middle shelf
Approximately 45 minutes

FINISHING

Greaseproof paper
Caster sugar

HAZELNUT CLUSTERS

1. Sift the flour into a bowl then mix in the oats, chopped hazelnuts and sugar.

2. Melt the margarine in a saucepan, beat the egg in a bowl then mix both into the dry ingredients together with the treacle. Mix until well blended.

3. Form into small rounds about 1cm (½in) thick, place onto the trays and bake.

INGREDIENTS
Makes 30

Metric		Imperial
115g	Plain flour	4oz
225g	Rolled oats	8oz
115g	Hazelnuts, chopped	4oz
115g	Light brown soft sugar	4oz
115g	Margarine	4oz
	1 egg, size 3	
15ml	Lyle's black treacle	1tbsp

BAKING TRAYS

Lightly greased baking trays.

BAKING

Preheated oven, 200°C or 400°F
or gas mark 5
Middle Shelf
15-20 minutes

Mary's Tips

Place a few sugar cubes with the biscuits in a tin to keep fresh and crisp.

GOLDEN OATIES

1. Gently melt the butter with the syrup in a saucepan. Mix the flour, sugar, oats and ginger in a mixing bowl.

2. Stir in the melted butter together with the water until well blended.

3. Leave to cool for 5 minutes then mould into balls and place well apart on the trays and bake. After a few minutes transfer the biscuits onto a wire tray to cool.

INGREDIENTS
Makes 30

Metric		Imperial
115g	Butter	4oz
30ml	Lyle's golden syrup	2tbsp
115g	Self-raising flour	4oz
115g	Light brown soft sugar	4oz
115g	Rolled oats	4oz
5ml	Ground ginger	1tsp
10ml	Water	2tsp

BAKING TRAYS

Well greased baking trays.

BAKING

Preheated oven, 150°C or 300°F or gas mark 2
Middle Shelf
Approximately 25 minutes

Mary's Tips

Measure golden syrup carefully. It will mix more readily with other ingredients if it slightly warmed.

ORANGE BARS

INGREDIENTS

Makes 16

Metric		Imperial
170g	Plain flour, sifted	6oz
60g	Semolina	2oz
85g	Caster sugar	3oz
170g	Butter or margarine	6oz
	Finely grated rind of 1 orange	

TOPPING

170g	Icing sugar, sifted	6oz
	Orange juice	

BAKING TIN

Well greased 18cm (7in) square, shallow baking tin.

BAKING

Preheated oven, 170°C, 340°F or gas mark 3
Middle shelf
Approximately 45 minutes or until firm to the touch, then add the topping and bake for a further 10 minutes

Mary's Tips

Do not overbake the topping.

Before grating, scrub the oranges to remove the wax coating. Use a coarse grater.

Lemon or lime can be used instead of orange for the biscuit and the topping.

1. Mix the flour, semolina and sugar together in a bowl. Rub the butter or margarine into the mixture to form breadcrumb texture. Mix in the grated orange rind.

2. Spoon the mixture into the tin and firm down evenly with a spatula and then bake. Meanwhile, mix the icing sugar and orange juice to make a thick coating consistency.

3. Spread over the biscuit when baked and return to the oven for 10 more minutes. Then leave in the tin to cool before cutting.

DIGESTIVE BISCUITS

INGREDIENTS

Makes 16

Metric		Imperial
100g	Wholemeal flour	3½oz
45g	Fine or medium oatmeal	1½oz
2.5ml	Baking powder	½tsp
	Pinch of salt	
60g	Soft margarine	2oz
15ml	Dark brown soft sugar	1tbsp
30-45ml	Milk	2-3tbsp

BAKING TRAYS

Well greased baking trays.

BAKING

Preheated oven, 180°C, 360°F or gas mark 4
Middle shelf
12-15 minutes or until just browning on the edges

Mary's Tips

For a sweet biscuit, coat one side with melted chocolate.

Comb the top as shown on page 89.

1. Thoroughly mix the flour, oatmeal, baking powder and salt in a bowl. Rub in the margarine until the mixture resembles breadcrumbs.

2. Stir in the sugar and milk using the blade of a knife. Combine together then knead lightly to a dough.

3. Roll out the dough on a floured surface to 3mm (⅛in) thick. Cut out rounds and place onto the trays. Prick with a fork and bake. Lift the biscuits onto a wire tray to cool.

TRADITIONAL BOURBON

INGREDIENTS
Makes 18

Metric		Imperial
115g	Margarine	4oz
85g	Caster sugar	3oz
60g	Lyle's golden syrup	2oz
15ml	Egg, beaten	1tbsp
170g	Plain flour	6oz
60g	Semolina	2oz
30g	Cocoa powder	1oz

TOPPING
30g	Granulated sugar	1oz

FILLING
115g	Butter	4oz
170g	Icing sugar, sifted	6oz
60g	Plain or milk Scotbloc or Chocolat	2oz

BAKING TRAY
Well greased baking trays.

BAKING
Preheated oven, 180°C, 360°F
or gas mark 4
Middle shelf
15 minutes

Mary's Tips

To make the buttercream filling, use butter at room temperature.
Beat the butter and icing sugar together until smooth and creamy.
Flavour as required.

1. *Cream the margarine, sugar and syrup together, then beat in the egg a little at a time.*

2. *Sift together the flour, semolina and cocoa powder, twice. Gradually fold into the creamed mixture.*

3. *Knead the mixture to form a smooth, well blended dough. Do not overmix.*

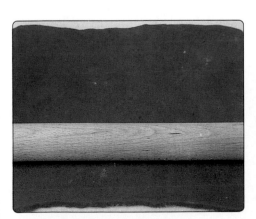

4. *Gently roll out the dough, into a square shape, on a lightly floured surface.*

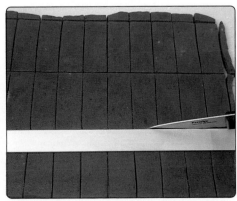

5. *Using a rule, cut into even sized fingers. Prick each one with a fork then sprinkle on the granulated sugar. Place slightly apart onto the trays and bake. Leave until cold.*

6. *For the filling, beat the butter until light then beat in the icing sugar. Quickly beat in the melted chocolate (see page 15). Sandwich the biscuits together with the filling.*

PARKIN

1. Sift the flour and spices together then mix in the oatmeal. Rub in the fat until an even, crumbly mixture is achieved.

2. Stir in the sugar and syrup then the bicarbonate of soda dissolved in 1tbsp of milk. Mix to a soft dough, using the remaining milk if required. Divide the mixture in half and roll to sausage shape.

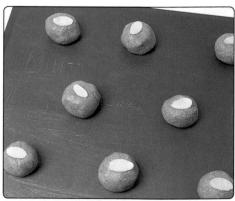

3. Cut each roll into 12 pieces. Roll into balls between floured hands and place onto trays. Place split almonds on top then bake. After baking leave to cool on trays.

INGREDIENTS
Makes 24

Metric		Imperial
170g	Plain flour	6oz
10ml	Ground ginger	2tsp
5ml	Ground cinnamon	1tsp
170g	Medium oatmeal	6oz
60g	Butter or margarine	2oz
60g	Light brown soft sugar	2oz
225g	Lyle's golden syrup	8oz
2.5ml	Bicarbonate of soda	½tsp
15-30ml	Milk	2tbsp

DECORATION

Split blanched almonds

BAKING TRAYS

Well greased baking trays.

BAKING

Preheated oven, 170°C, 340°F
or gas mark 3
Middle shelf
20 minutes or until golden brown

POLKA DOTS

1. Sift the flour into a mixing bowl then add the fat, sugar and eggs. Beat with a wooden spoon for 4 minutes, or with an electric beater for 2 minutes.

2. Fold in the coconut, milk and essence until well blended. Gently fold in the sugar coated chocolate drops.

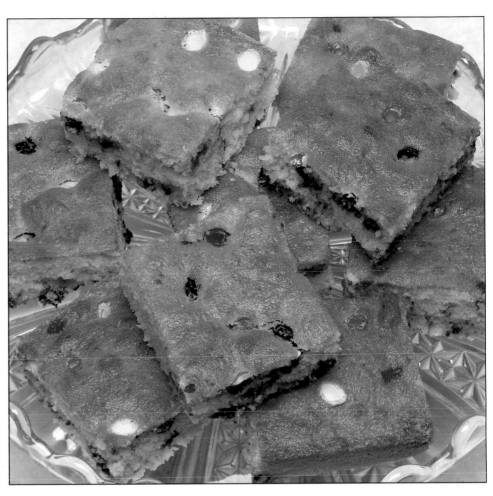

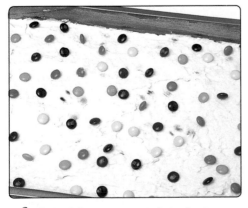

3. Spread the mixture evenly in the tin. Sprinkle chocolate drops on top and bake. After baking leave for 2-3 minutes before turning out onto a wire tray to cool. Cut into squares.

INGREDIENTS
Makes 16

Metric		Imperial
145g	Self-raising flour	5oz
115g	Margarine or butter, softened	4oz
115g	Caster sugar	4oz
	2 eggs, size 3	
60g	Dessicated coconut	2oz
2.5ml	Vanilla essence	½tsp
30ml	Milk	2tbsp
60g	Sugar coated chocolate drops	2oz

DECORATION

30g	Sugar coated chocolate drops	1oz

BAKING TIN

Greased and floured 18 x 28cm (7 x 11in) shallow baking tin.

BAKING

Preheated oven, 180°C, 360°F or gas mark 4
Middle shelf
25-30 minutes or until springy to the touch

Mary's Tips

Mix in the sugar coated chocolate drops as quickly as possible to avoid the coloured sugar dissolving in the mixture.

Chocolate drops can be used instead of sugar coated drops.

COCONUT BARS

1. To make the base, sift the flour into a bowl, add the margarine and rub between fingers until mixture resembles breadcrumbs. Mix in the sugar.

2. Add about 30ml (2tbsp) of water and mix with a knife then knead to form a pastry. Roll out and fit into the tin, prick with a fork then bake for 20 minutes.

3. For the filling, whisk the eggs, brown sugar and essence together in a bowl until light and fluffy.

4. Sift the flour, salt and baking powder together then fold into the mixture with the coconut to form a crumbly texture.

Mary's Tips

Use cream cheese, icing sugar and lemon juice as an alternative topping.

When toasting coconut, watch it closely to avoid burning.

5. Spread onto the cooked base and lightly press evenly with a spatula. Bake in the oven for 10 minutes then leave in the tin until cold.

6. For the topping, toast the coconut until golden brown. Sift the icing sugar into a large bowl, melt the margarine and stir into the icing sugar with the lemon juice.

7. Spread over the top using a serrated scraper or fork to create a wavy pattern. Sprinkle with the toasted coconut then cut into squares.

INGREDIENTS
Makes 24

Metric		Imperial
145g	Plain flour	5oz
85g	Margarine	3oz
85g	Caster sugar	3oz
	Cold water to mix	

TOPPING

30g	Desiccated coconut	1oz
225g	Icing sugar	8oz
30g	Margarine	1oz
30ml	Lemon juice	2tbsp

FILLING

	2 eggs, size 3	
60g	Light brown soft sugar	2oz
5ml	Vanilla essence	1tsp
60g	Plain flour	2oz
1.25ml	Salt	¼tsp
7.5ml	Baking powder	1½tsp
285g	Desiccated coconut	10oz

BAKING TIN

Well greased 18 x 28cm (7 x 11in) shallow baking tin.

BAKING

Preheated oven, 180°C, 360°F or gas mark 4
Middle shelf
Bake the base for 20 minutes or until golden brown, add the filling then continue baking for 10 minutes.

COFFEE DROPS

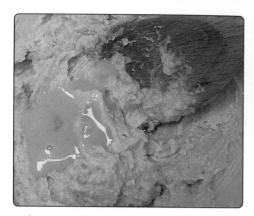

1. Cream the margarine, sugar and syrup together. Beat in the egg then the coffee essence.

2. Sift the flour and cinnamon together then gradually blend into the mixture to form a soft, smooth dough.

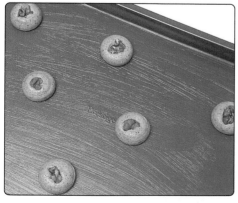

3. Fill a savoy bag and piping tube and then pipe small bulbs, well placed apart, onto the trays. Top with walnut pieces and bake.

INGREDIENTS

Makes 36

Metric		Imperial
60g	Margarine	2oz
60g	Light brown soft sugar	2oz
85g	Lyle's golden syrup	3oz
15ml	Egg, beaten	1tbsp
10ml	Coffee essence	2tsp
85g	Self-raising flour	3oz
2.5ml	Ground cinnamon	½tsp

DECORATION

Broken walnuts (optional)

BAKING TRAYS

Well greased baking trays.

BAKING

Preheated oven, 180°C, 360°F
or gas mark 4
Middle Shelf
Approximately 15 minutes

Mary's Tips

Extra care is needed when baking these biscuits as they will brown very quickly, especially when using a fan oven.

86

VIIKUNAKAKKU

1. Beat the butter and sugar together until light and fluffy. Whisk together the eggs and rind then gradually beat into the mixture, adding a little flour to stop mixture separating.

2. Sift the flour and baking powder together twice. Mix the fruit in 30ml (2tbsp) of the flour and fold into the creamed mixture then stir in the remaining flour.

3. Spread evenly into the tin and bake. After baking leave in the tin for 10 minutes then out onto a wire tray to cool. When cold, dust with icing sugar and cut into bars.

INGREDIENTS
Makes 24

Metric		Imperial
170g	Butter	6oz
115g	Light brown soft sugar	4oz
	3 eggs, size 2	
30ml	Orange rind, grated	2tbsp
170g	Plain flour	6oz
5ml	Baking powder	1tsp
70g	Dried figs, chopped	2½oz
70g	Seedless raisins	2½oz
30g	Walnuts, chopped	1oz

DECORATION

Icing sugar for dusting

BAKING TIN

Well grease then dust with caster sugar a 18 x 28cm (7 x 11in) shallow baking tin.

BAKING

Preheated oven, 180°C, 360°F or gas mark 4
Middle Shelf
40-45 minutes

Mary's Tips

This traybake is traditionally made in a ring mould.

Always use a very well greased tin.

GINGERBREAD SNAPS

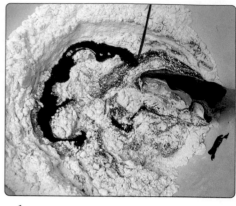

1. *Put the treacle, butter and sugar into a small saucepan. Stir over low heat until the butter has melted. Sift the remaining ingredients together into a bowl.*

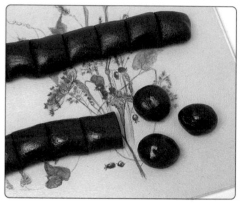

2. *When the treacle has cooled mix into the dry ingredients to form a soft, smooth dough. Turn out and divide in half. Roll to 25.5cm (10in) long and cut each into 10 pieces.*

INGREDIENTS
Makes 20

Metric		Imperial
90ml	Lyle's black treacle	**6tbsp**
85g	Butter	3oz
60g	Light brown soft sugar	2oz
225g	Plain flour	8oz
2.5ml	Ground ginger	½tsp
2.5ml	Ground coriander	½tsp
1.25ml	Bicarbonate of soda	¼tsp

TOPPINGS

Desiccated coconut
Demerara sugar
Oatmeal
Flaked almonds
Ginger pieces

BAKING TRAYS

Well greased baking trays.

BAKING

Preheated oven, 180°C, 360°F
or gas mark 4
Just above middle shelf
8-10 minutes

Mary's Tips

When measuring the treacle ensure it is level in the spoon with the bottom of the spoon scraped clean.

In step 1, make sure the heat is low as the mixture should melt not cook.

3. *Roll into balls and then into any of the suggested toppings, place onto trays and bake.*

FLORENTINES

INGREDIENTS
Makes 20

Metric		Imperial
85g	Plain flour, sifted	3oz
60g	Sultanas	2oz
115g	Glacé cherries, chopped	4oz
170g	Flaked almonds	6oz
170g	Lyle's golden syrup	6oz
170g	Butter	6oz

DECORATION

225g	Plain or milk Scotbloc or Chocolat	8oz

BAKING TRAYS

Baking trays of appropriate sizes with paper cases.

BAKING

Preheated oven, 190°C, 375°F
or gas mark 5
Middle shelf
10-12 minutes

Mary's Tips

If paper cases are not used,
watch the edges do not burn.

1. Mix together the flour, sultanas, glacé cherries and flaked almonds in a bowl. Place the syrup and butter into a saucepan and melt.

2. As soon as the butter has melted remove from the heat and stir in the mixed ingredients until well blended.

3. Spread small amounts into the baking cases or directly onto trays (see Mary's Tips) and bake. Leave to cool on the trays then coat the undersides with melted chocolate.

ALMOND and MINCEMEAT FINGERS

1. Place fat and sugar into a bowl. Separate the egg then add the yolk. Add essence then mix to form a smooth paste. Work in most of the egg white – reserving 1 teaspoon.

2. Mix together the flour and ground almonds then add to the mixture. Mix until a smooth pastry is formed.

INGREDIENTS
Makes 14

Metric		Imperial
85g	Butter or margarine	3oz
85g	Caster sugar	3oz
	1 egg, size 3	
	2 drops almond essence	
170g	Plain flour	6oz
85g	Ground almonds	3oz

FILLING

225g	Mincemeat	8oz
	Grated rind of 1 small lemon.	

TOPPING

30g	Flaked almonds	1oz

BAKING TIN

Well greased 18 x 28cm (7 x 11in) shallow baking tin.

BAKING

Preheated oven, 180°C, 360°F or gas mark 4
Middle shelf
Approximately 20 minutes

3. Divide the pastry in half, roll out and press into the base of the tin.

4. Spread the mincemeat on top then the grated lemon rind.

5. Roll out the remaining pastry and lightly press onto the top. Brush with the remaining egg white and sprinkle on the flaked almonds.

6. Leave in a cool place for 30 minutes. Mark into 14 fingers then bake. After baking gently lift out the fingers onto a wire tray to cool.

Mary's Tips

For variations of the filling add a little cooked apple to the mincemeat. Or use 450g (1lb) cooked apples with 60g (2oz) of sultanas instead of the mincemeat.

MONKEY PUZZLES

1. Sift together the flour and cocoa powder, twice. Cream the margarine and syrup until soft.

2. Stir in the flour. Coarsely crush the cornflakes and stir into the mixture until well blended.

3. Place spoonfuls, walnut size, onto greased trays and bake. When cold, dip tops into melted chocolate (see page 15) and decorate as required.

INGREDIENTS

Makes 20

Metric		Imperial
70g	Plain flour	2½oz
22.5ml	Cocoa powder	1½tbsp
85g	Margarine	3oz
85g	Lyle's golden syrup	3oz
30g	Crisp cornflakes	1oz

DECORATION

Plain or milk Scotbloc or Chocolat, melted
White Scotbloc, melted

BAKING TRAYS

Well greased baking trays.

BAKING

Preheated oven, 180°C, 360°F or gas mark 4
Middle Shelf
Approximately 12 minutes

Mary's Tips

To drizzle chocolate, fill a small piping bag and cut a tiny hole at the tip. Squeeze gently and move backwards and forwards.

CRISPY OVALS

INGREDIENTS

Makes 24

Metric		Imperial
	2 rashers back bacon	
115g	Plain wholemeal flour	**4oz**
1.25ml	Ground coriander	**¼tsp**
	Good pinch of cayenne pepper	
85g	Butter	**3oz**
85g	Matured Cheddar cheese, grated	**3oz**
15-20ml	Milk	**3-4tsp**
15ml	Lyle's golden syrup	**1tbsp**
	Milk for glazing	

Sesame seeds
Poppy seeds
Parmesan cheese, grated

BAKING TRAYS

Well greased baking trays.

BAKING

Preheated oven, 190°C, 375°F
or gas mark 5
Middle Shelf
10 minutes or until lightly browned

Mary's Tips

Other savoury toppings could be used such as anchovies or roasted chopped peppers.

For cocktail biscuits, use a small cutter.

These biscuits make an excellent base for hors d'oevres.

1. Derind the bacon, cut into pieces and fry until very crisp. Drain on kitchen paper. Sift the flour, coriander and pepper together then mix in the butter forming a crumb texture.

2. Chop the bacon finely then add to the mixture with the cheese. Mix together to form a pliable dough, adding sufficient milk as required.

3. Roll the dough on surface dusted with wholemeal flour. Cut into fluted ovals and place onto the trays. Brush with milk, sprinkle on various toppings and bake.

CHRISTMAS COOKIES

1. Place the margarine or butter, sugar, sifted flour, milk and syrup into a bowl. Mix the ingredients together, using a wooden spoon or electric beater, until it forms a soft dough.

2. Turn out onto lightly floured surface and knead. Gently roll out the dough and cut shapes as required.

INGREDIENTS

Metric		Imperial
115g	Soft tub margarine or Butter	4oz
145g	Caster sugar	5oz
225g	Plain flour, sifted	8oz
45ml	Milk	3tbsp
15ml	Lyle's golden syrup	1tbsp

DECORATION

A little royal icing
Plain or milk Scotbloc or Chocolat, melted

BAKING TRAYS

Well greased baking trays.

BAKING

Preheated oven, 190°C, 375°F
or gas mark 5
Middle shelf
15 minutes or until pale golden in colour

Mary's Tips

Do not overknead the dough as otherwise a tough biscuit will result.

Wrap the cookies in coloured foil and hang on the Christmas tree.

3. Place onto the greased trays and bake. After baking leave for 5 minutes then cool on wire trays. Decorate with chocolate for feet and royal icing for the snow.

SANTA'S BISCUITS

INGREDIENTS
Makes 30

Metric		Imperial
115g	Butter	4oz
115g	Caster sugar	4oz
	1 egg, size 2, lightly beaten	
225g	Plain flour	8oz
	Pinch of salt	
	Grated rind of 1 small orange	

DECORATION

A little sugarpaste and royal icing

BAKING TRAYS

Well greased baking trays.

BAKING

Preheated oven, 180°C, 360°F
or gas mark 4
Middle shelf
15 minutes or until pale golden in
colour

Mary's Tips

Sugarpaste can be purchased
from most supermarkets.

1. Cream the butter and sugar until light, white and fluffy. Thoroughly beat in the egg, a little at a time.

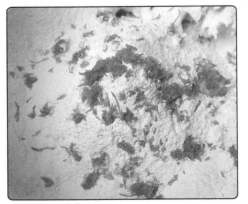

2. Sift the flour and salt together twice, then gently fold into the mixture with the grated orange rind. Mix to a firm dough.

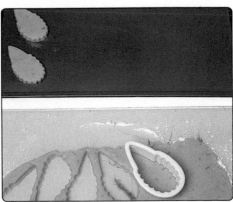

3. Wrap in greaseproof paper and chill for 30 minutes. Roll out, not too thin, cut shapes required and bake. When baked, leave on a wire tray to cool then decorate as required.

MARY FORD TITLES

101 Cake Designs
ISBN: 0 946429 00 6   320 pages
The original Mary Ford cake artistry text book. A classic in its field, over 200,000 copies sold.

Cake Making and Decorating
ISBN: 0 946429 41 3   96 pages
Mary Ford divulges all the skills and techniques cake decorators need to make and decorate a variety of cakes in every medium.

Jams, Chutneys and Pickles
ISBN: 0 946429 48 0   96 pages
Over 70 of Mary Ford's favourite recipes for delicious jams, jellies, pickles and chutneys with hints and tips for perfect results.

Children's Cakes
ISBN: 0 946429 35 9   96 pages
33 exciting new Mary Ford designs and templates for children's cakes in a wide range of mediums.

Children's Birthday Cakes
ISBN: 0 946429 46 4   112 pages
The book to have next to you in the kitchen! Over forty new cake ideas for children's cakes with an introduction on cake making and baking to ensure the cake is both delicious as well as admired.

Party Cakes
ISBN: 0 946429 13 8   120 pages
36 superb party time sponge cake designs and templates for tots to teenagers. An invaluable prop for the party cake decorator.

Quick and Easy Cakes
ISBN: 0 946429 42 1   208 pages
The book for the busy mum. 99 new ideas for party and special occasion cakes.

Decorative Sugar Flowers for Cakes
ISBN: 0 946429 51 0   120 pages
33 of the highest quality handcrafted sugar flowers with cutter shapes, background information and appropriate uses.

Cake Recipes
ISBN: 0 946429 43 X   96 pages
Contains 60 of Mary's favourite cake recipes ranging from fruit cake to cinnamon crumble cake.

One Hundred Easy Cake Designs
ISBN: 0 946429 47 2   208 pages
Mary Ford has originated 100 cakes all of which have been selected for ease and speed of making. The ideal book for the busy parent or friend looking for inspiration for a special occasion cake.

Sugarcraft Cake Decorating
ISBN: 0 946429 30 8   96 pages
A definitive sugarcraft book featuring an extensive selection of exquisite sugarcraft items designed and made by Pat Ashby.

Wedding Cakes
ISBN: 0 946429 39 1   96 pages
For most cake decorators, the wedding cake is the most complicated item they will produce. This book gives a full step-by-step description of the techniques required and includes over 20 new cake designs.

Home Baking with Chocolate
ISBN: 0 946429 37 5   96 pages
Over 60 tried and tested recipes for cakes, gateaux, biscuits, confectionery and desserts. The ideal book for busy mothers.

Making Cakes for Money
ISBN: 0 946429 44 8   120 pages
The complete guide to making and costing cakes for sale at stalls or to friends. Invaluable advice on costing ingredients and time accurately.

The Complete Book of Cake Decorating
ISBN: 0 946429 36 7   256 pages
An indispensable reference book for cake decorators, containing totally new material covering every aspect of cake design and artistry.

The Beginners Guide to Cake Decorating
ISBN: 0 946429 38 3   256 pages
A comprehensive guide for the complete beginner to every stage of the cake decorating process, including over 150 cake designs for different occasions.

Desserts
ISBN: 0 946429 40 5   96 pages
Hot and cold desserts suitable for every occasion, using fresh, natural ingredients. An invaluable reference book for the home cook, chef or student.

The New Book of Cake Decorating
ISBN: 0 9462429 45 6   224 pages
The most comprehensive title in the Mary Ford list. It includes over 100 new cake designs and full descriptions of all the latest techniques.

BOOKS BY MAIL ORDER

Mary Ford operates a mail order service for all her step-by-step titles. If you write to Mary at the address below she will provide you with a price list and details. In addition, all names on the list receive information on new books and special offers. Mary is delighted, if required, to write a personal message in any book purchased by mail order.

Write to: Mary Ford,
            30 Duncliff Road,
            Southbourne, Bournemouth,
            Dorset. BH6 4LJ. U.K.